DATE DUE

# Amazing
# AFRICA
## PROJECTS
## You Can
## Build
## Yourself

**Build It Yourself Series**

green press INITIATIVE

Nomad Press is committed to preserving ancient forests and natural resources. We elected to print *Amazing Africa Projects You Can Build Yourself* on 4,007 lbs. of Williamsburg Recycled 30% offset.

Nomad Press made this paper choice because our printer, Sheridan Books, is a member of Green Press Initiative, a nonprofit program dedicated to supporting authors, publishers, and suppliers in their efforts to reduce their use of fiber obtained from endangered forests. For more information, visit www.greenpressinitiative.org

Nomad Press
A division of Nomad Communications
10 9 8 7 6 5 4 3 2 1
Copyright © 2010 by Nomad Press
All rights reserved.

This book was manufactured by Sheridan Books,
Ann Arbor, MI USA
February 2010, Job #313445
ISBN: 978-1-9346704-1-5

Illustrations by Megan Stearns; Dover Publications, Inc.

Questions regarding the ordering of this book should be addressed to
Independent Publishers Group
814 N. Franklin St.
Chicago, IL 60610
www.ipgbook.com

Nomad Press
2456 Christian St.
White River Junction, VT 05001
www.nomadpress.net

# CONTENTS

## Introduction
One Continent, Many Worlds 1

### Chapter 1
Natural Wonders 4

### Chapter 2
Minerals 13

### Chapter 3
Wildlife 22

### Chapter 4
Great Civilizations 32

### Chapter 5
Hunters, Herders, and Farmers 39

### Chapter 6
Ethnic Groups 49

### Chapter 7
Homes 59

### Chapter 8
Food & Daily Life 65

### Chapter 9
Games & Toys 75

### Chapter 10
Clothing & Adornment 81

### Chapter 11
Music 88

### Chapter 12
Ceremonies & Masks 95

### Chapter 13
Language & Storytelling 103

### Chapter 14
Overcoming Challenges 111

## Glossary ❖ Index

# TIMELINE OF AFRICA'S HISTORY

## Ancient Africa, c. 200,000-10,000 BCE
- Homo sapiens live in East Africa and form nomadic groups.
- Homo sapiens develop the earliest known stone tools.
- The nomadic San people spread throughout southern Africa.

## Early Civilizations, c. 10,000 BCE-0 CE
- River settlements emerge on the Nile, Niger, and Congo Rivers.
- Ancient Egyptian civilization flourishes along the Nile. They build the Great Pyramids and develop a hieroglyphic system of writing.
- The Kush, or Nubian, empire rises to power and rivals Ancient Egypt in wealth, power, and culture.

## African Empires, c. 0-1400 CE
- The Axum Empire becomes a Christian kingdom.
- Bananas and yams from Southeast Asia reach Africa.
- Use of iron spreads in Africa.
- Islam sweeps across North Africa.
- The Bantu people migrate from West Africa into Central and Southern Africa. It is the largest human migration in history.
- Arab slave trade begins. Historians estimate around 14 million Africans were sold into slavery during this time.
- Gold trade grows across the Sahara. Several Western African kingdoms (Ghana, Mali, and Songhai) thrive and grow wealthy.
- The Shona people build the Great Zimbabwe stone walls and buildings.

## European Exploration and the Atlantic Slave Trade, c. 1400-1870 CE

- Portuguese explorers reach West Africa's Gold Coast.
- Benin Empire in West Africa reaches height of power.
- Portuguese capture first Africans and sell them as slaves. They also trade goods to African groups in exchange for more Africans to enslave.
- Portuguese trade in Africa attracts other European nations.
- Discovery of the Americas and Caribbean islands. Growth of plantations increases the demand for slave labor. The era of the Atlantic slave trade begins.
- Dutch establish colony at the Cape of Good Hope in South Africa. Large Dutch farms push out the San people.
- Asante Empire formed under first King Osei Tutu. The Asante grow rich and powerful trading gold and people to European traders in exchange for firearms.
- Atlantic slave trade reaches its peak between 1650 and 1800. Historians estimate over 9 million enslaved people completed the journey across the Atlantic Ocean. Millions more died during the crossings.

## The Colonial Period, c. 1800-1950 CE

- Abolitionist movement grows in Europe and the Americas. Europe bans slave trade in early 1800s and then practice of slavery. The United States officially bans slavery in 1865.
- Children discover a 21-carat diamond on the banks of the Orange River. Diamond prospectors descend on South Africa.
- Rich gold deposits found in the Witwatersrand hills of South Africa in 1884. The African gold rush begins.
- The Scramble for Africa begins in 1885. Europe rushes to colonize Africa. By 1910, Europe rules almost the entire continent.

## Independence, c. 1950-present

- Ghana becomes first African nation to earn independence in 1957. Other African nations follow.
- South Africa becomes the last African nation to become an independent free state in 1994. President F.W. deClerk outlaws apartheid.

# OTHER TITLES FROM NOMAD PRESS

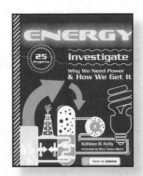

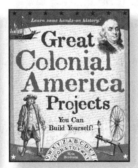

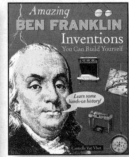

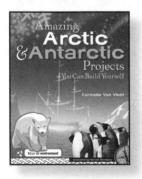

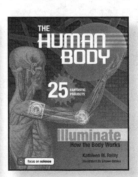

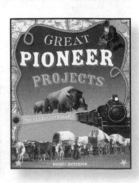

# ONE CONTINENT, MANY WORLDS

**H**ave you ever wondered what it would be like to visit Africa? Often shrouded in mystery, Africa is home to many spectacular sights. You could sail down the world's longest river or cross the largest desert. You might trek through a rainforest and marvel at the mist from the world's biggest waterfall.

On the **savanna**, you'll find thundering elephants and towering giraffes. If you're lucky, you might even catch a glimpse of a lion stalking his **prey**. Rising above the savanna, the snow-capped peaks of Mt. Kilimanjaro, Africa's highest mountain, offer another adventure.

Africa is more than just scenery and **wildlife**. It is thought to be the birthplace of humankind. The world's oldest human **fossils** were discovered in Africa.

It was here that our common **ancestors** first lived and thrived. They built great **civilizations** and created art and music. They established traditions in ceremonies and storytelling that were passed down for generations. Everywhere you look in Africa, from a Maasai warrior's red shuka to the awesome stone walls of Great Zimbabwe, a piece of history remains.

From rural villages to bustling modern cities, Africa is one of the most **diverse** places on Earth. The variety of **climates**, landscapes, people, plants, and animals is staggering.

## WORDS TO KNOW

**savanna:** wide open, grassy area.

**prey:** an animal hunted for food.

**wildlife:** wild animals and birds.

**fossil:** the remains of an ancient plant or animal preserved in rock.

**ancestor:** people from your family or country that lived before you.

**civilization:** a highly developed society.

**diverse:** when there are many different kinds of something.

**climate:** average weather patterns in an area over a period of many years.

**minerals:** the crystal structures in rocks.

**colonization:** when one country settles in another country and takes over.

---

**Today's Africa is much more than a single continent. It is 53 nations, each with its own culture and traditions.**

---

This book will visit some of Africa's natural wonders and explore its wildlife and **mineral** resources. You'll learn about many of Africa's traditions, from music and ceremonies to storytelling and masked dances. This book also explores some of Africa's past, from its great ancient civilizations to the Atlantic slave trade and European **colonization**. This book will help you better understand what life in much of Africa is like.

Most of the projects in this book can be made with little adult supervision, using materials you already have at home. So take a deep breath and get ready to visit Africa!

# AFRICA

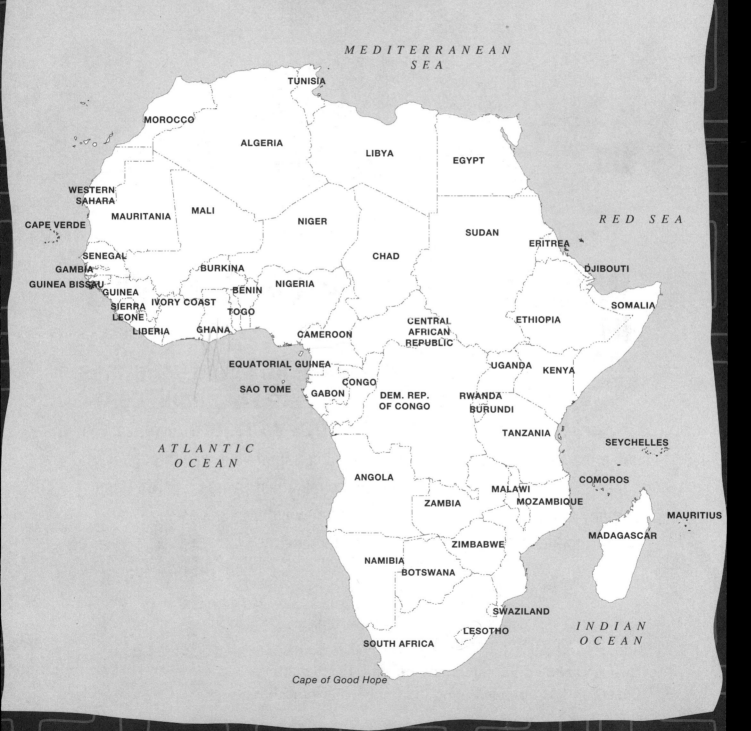

*MEDITERRANEAN SEA*

TUNISIA

MOROCCO

ALGERIA

LIBYA

EGYPT

*RED SEA*

WESTERN SAHARA

MAURITANIA

MALI

NIGER

SUDAN

ERITREA

DJIBOUTI

CAPE VERDE

SENEGAL

GAMBIA

GUINEA BISSAU

GUINEA

SIERRA LEONE

LIDERIA

IVORY COAST

GHANA

BURKINA

BENIN

TOGO

NIGERIA

CAMEROON

CENTRAL AFRICAN REPUBLIC

ETHIOPIA

SOMALIA

EQUATORIAL GUINEA

SAO TOME

GABON

CONGO

DEM. REP. OF CONGO

UGANDA

KENYA

RWANDA

BURUNDI

TANZANIA

SEYCHELLES

*ATLANTIC OCEAN*

ANGOLA

ZAMBIA

MALAWI

MOZAMBIQUE

COMOROS

MAURITIUS

MADAGASCAR

ZIMBABWE

NAMIBIA

BOTSWANA

SWAZILAND

LESOTHO

*INDIAN OCEAN*

SOUTH AFRICA

*Cape of Good Hope*

### Chapter 1

# NATURAL WONDERS

**S**ome things in nature, like towering waterfalls and soaring mountains, are so magnificent that we call them natural wonders. In Africa, you can cross mile after mile of dry desert. You can fight your way through a dense rainforest, or travel down one of the mightiest rivers on Earth. Home to many of the world's most amazing natural wonders, Africa sparkles with nature's raw power and beauty.

## The Nile River

Known as the world's longest river, the Nile is about 4,200 miles (6,800 kilometers) long. It winds through nine different countries and the **Sahara Desert** until it reaches Egypt and the Mediterranean Sea.

The Nile **River basin** is enormous, taking up about one-tenth of the African continent. It is also ancient. The Nile has flowed through Africa in different forms for 30 million years.

The Nile is an important source of water and life in Africa. For thousands of years, people and civilizations have thrived on the banks of the Nile. They have used the river's rich banks for farming and its abundant waters for fishing. The Nile's **fertile** soil results from heavy rains in Ethiopia causing the river to flood its banks. The flooding leaves behind rich, black **sediment** that is good for growing **crops**.

Ancient Egypt was the most famous civilization along the Nile River. The Nile supported Egyptian civilization with fertile farmland so there was plenty of food. Recognizing the river's importance, the Egyptians worshipped the river and its **delta** as the God Hapi. It was believed that Hapi controlled the Nile's annual flooding and renewal of rich soil.

The Nile is just as important to life in Africa today. The constant source of water allows farmers to grow crops even in Africa's high temperatures and dry desert. Modern dams built along the river control irrigation and the natural flooding of the Nile.

As countries along the river basin develop, some people fear conflict may arise over access to this amazing, life-sustaining river.

In addition to human settlements, many animals, birds, and fish rely on the Nile for life. There are over 100 different **species** of fish swimming in the Nile River. Birds like flamingos and scarlet ibis gather near its waters. Crocodiles and hippos lurk beneath the surface. And land animals such as wildebeest and baboons come to the Nile to drink.

The Nile River flows through nine countries: Burundi, Kenya, Republic of Congo (formerly Zaire), Rwanda, Tanzania, Uganda, Sudan, Ethiopia, and Egypt.

# The Sahara Desert

Did you know that a **desert** can be hot or cold? The largest desert in the world is actually a cold desert, covering the continent of Antarctica with snow and ice. Africa's Sahara is the largest hot desert in the world. It's almost as big as the United States, covering 3.5 million square miles (5.6 million square kilometers) of North Africa. It stretches from the Atlantic Ocean to the Red Sea.

Many people picture shifting sand and waves of golden dunes when they think of the Sahara. In fact, sand and dunes cover only one quarter of it. The most common feature of the Sahara is its stony plains. Gravel covers some areas, while others have been swept clean of sand and fine gravel by fierce winds.

The Sahara is one of the harshest places in the world. Temperatures can reach 120 degrees Fahrenheit (49 degrees Celsius). At night temperatures can drop below freezing (32 degrees Fahrenheit or 0 degrees Celsius). Rainfall is scarce, and dry winds often kick up sand or dust storms.

The winds can carry so much dust and sand that an approaching storm can look like a mile-high wall of dust.

Despite these harsh conditions, plants, animals, and people live in the Sahara. To survive here, you must be able to adapt to the desert's high heat and unpredictable rainfall. Grasses, shrubs, and trees that grow on the dry plains need little water. Animals such as the desert hedgehog, sand fox, and mongoose gather near scarce water and plants. The Saharan people generally lead a **nomadic** life. They move often, looking for water and food.

## WORDS TO KNOW

**species:** a type of animal or plant.

**desert:** a landscape or region with very little precipitation (rain or snow).

**nomadic:** a life of moving around.

**archaeologist:** a scientist who studies ancient people and their cultures.

**artifact:** a simple object like a tool or piece of pottery from a culture.

**biodiverse:** a lot of different forms of life in an area.

**Archaeologists** believe that centuries ago, the Sahara's climate was not as harsh as it is today. They have found fossils and **artifacts** that show many people used to live there. As the Sahara's climate changed over time, people moved to regions with better farming conditions and weather.

# The African Rainforest

In stark contrast to the dry Sahara, the African rainforest is very warm and humid. Some areas get as much as 400 inches (1,000 centimeters) of rain each year. After the Amazon rainforest, the African rainforest is the second largest rainforest in the world. Located mostly in central Africa, the rainforest covers about 400,000 square miles (644,000 square kilometers).

The rainforest is one of the most **biodiverse** places in the world. Half of Africa's animals and over 2,000 species of plants live and grow here. The highest layer in the rainforest is called the emergent layer. This is at the tops of towering hardwood trees that can grow over 200 feet tall (61 meters). A few birds and insects live in these huge trees, which soak up most of the sun and wind.

**Mongoose**

Beneath the emergent layer lies the canopy. The trees here rise 60 to 90 feet (18 to 27 meters) above the ground and form a roof over the rainforest. Most rainforest animals live in this leafy layer. Birds, insects, monkeys, and reptiles scamper through the maze of leaves and branches looking for food. Thick, snake-like vines twist among the canopy's trees.

**Daab Lizard**

Plants such as moss, lichens, and orchids grow on the trunks and branches of canopy trees. These plants are called epiphytes or air plants. Epiphytes grow using **nutrients** from the air and rain.

Living on canopy trees gives the epiphytes more direct sunlight. They can spread their seeds using canopy animals or the wind. Epiphytes also provide food, water, and shelter for many canopy animals. Stiff, upturned leaves or flowers can hold pools of water. Some species of insect larvae and frog tadpoles grow in this water. Canopy birds may drop in to drink the water and feast on the insect larvae. The epiphytes, in turn, get nutrients from the waste of their inhabitants.

**Orchids**

# DEFORESTATION

The African rainforest is disappearing at an alarming rate. When logging companies cut down trees for wood, or farmers clear land for crops, it destroys valuable resources. Animals and plants that lose their rainforest home are at risk of becoming **extinct**. Also, rainforest trees take in **carbon dioxide** from the air and release oxygen that we breathe. Decreasing this balance may upset the Earth's **atmosphere**.

The African rainforest also contains plants that we can use to make life-saving medicines. For example, the rosy periwinkle from Madagascar gives us a drug called vincristine that is used to treat leukemia patients. Researchers are currently studying rainforest plants to find more possible cures for AIDS, cancer, and other diseases. As these plants die, we may never have the chance to discover a new life-saving medicine.

The next layer down is the understory. Many insects live in the understory's small trees and short, leafy shrubs, along with some birds, snakes, and small mammals. Because the canopy above is so thick, very little sunlight reaches the understory. The understory's trees and shrubs have had to **adapt** to living in this dark and humid environment.

**Rainforest of Central Africa**

 **10 percent of Africa's rainforest plants can't be found anywhere else in the world.**

## WORDS TO KNOW

**nutrients:** the substances in food and soil that animals and plants need to grow.

**extinct:** when an entire species dies.

**carbon dioxide:** a gas created when animals breathe and when plants and animals rot or something is burned.

**atmosphere:** the gases that surround the earth.

**adapt:** changes a plant or animal makes to survive in new or different conditions.

The forest floor is a dense tangle of roots. Large tree trunks, hanging vines, and some ground plants litter the forest floor. It is almost always completely shaded, unless a fallen tree creates a small opening for sunlight. Larger rainforest animals like the forest elephant, leopard, and aardvark can be found here.

Leaves on the dark, humid floor decay quickly into the soil. Any nutrients from the decayed leaves are quickly absorbed by the roots of living plants and trees, continuing the rainforest's cycle of life.

# Victoria Falls

South of the rainforest, you can see mist rising off of Victoria Falls from 40 miles away. This magnificent South African waterfall is a 1-mile-wide (1,700-meter) curtain of water as it drops over the cliffs. Victoria Falls is two times higher than Niagara Falls. It is said that the noise made by the falls is greater than a million migrating wildebeests. The local African people named this wonder Mosi-Oa-Tunya or "the smoke that thunders."

**Aardvark**

At the top of the falls, the Zambezi River swells before plunging over 350 feet (107 meters) into the gorge below. Spray from the falls soars over 1,000 feet (305 meters) into the sky. The falls create a delicate, endless shower of rain and rainbows. Even at night a bright moon illuminates rainbows in the mist. In the early morning and late afternoon, the water and mist reflect the pink and orange hues of dawn and dusk.

# The Great Rift Valley

Deep underground, the African earth is slowly pulling apart like a zipper. Movement and shifting of the earth's crust causes this **rifting**. Over thousands of years, rifting action has caused large chunks of crust to sink, forming Africa's Great Rift Valley. As the crust shifted and separated, it also thinned. **Magma** rose through the separations in the thinned crust to form rift volcanoes. Today, the valley's active and semi-active volcanoes and hot boiling springs tell scientists that underground activity is still occurring.

# NGORONGORO CRATER

Millions of years ago, the Ngorongoro volcano was one of the world's tallest mountains. Then the volcano exploded and its center collapsed. This collapse formed a large, basin-like depression in the earth called a **caldera**. The Ngorongoro Crater is located in Tanzania. It is 12 miles wide and the largest unbroken volcanic caldera in the world.

Ngorongoro's floor sits 2,000 feet (610 meters) below the rim. Known as Africa's "Garden of Eden," the crater is a wildlife paradise. Thirty thousand animals live protected by the crater walls, including lions, elephants, wildebeests, zebra, rhinos, gazelles, and buffalo.

The Great Rift Valley stretches 5,000 miles (8,046 kilometers) from Mozambique in south-eastern Africa to Syria in the Middle East. The rift is so deep and defined in Kenya that it can be seen clearly from Space. It has low plains, steep hillsides, rocky volcanic areas, and lakes. In fact, the great lakes of East Africa, including Lake Victoria, formed in and around the Rift Valley.

Mount Kilimanjaro is the tallest mountain in Africa, 19,000 feet (5,800 meters) high. It is also an inactive volcano. Unlike many places in Africa, snow caps the peaks of Mount Kilimanjaro. Scientists believe, however, that the snow is melting because of rising temperatures. Some say that the snows of Mount Kilimanjaro could disappear within 20 years.

The Rift Valley is a rich source of fossils. Scientists have found fossils of some of the earliest human ancestors in a steep ravine called Olduvai Gorge, located in Tanzania. British scientist Mary Leakey also discovered a three-million-year-old fossilized footprint of a human ancestor that proved they walked upright. Other researchers have found evidence of crude shelters, weapons, and basic tools. The fossils have led some scientists to believe that the human race originated in East Africa.

The Great Rift Valley is not the only place where scientists believe rifting has affected Africa. **Geologists** think that long ago the African and Arabian coasts were connected. Rifting split them apart and the Red Sea filled the rift. Some geologists predict that if Africa's Great Rift Valley continues to grow it will eventually split the continent.

## WORDS TO KNOW

**rifting:** to split open or break apart.

**magma:** melted rock in the earth's crust.

**caldera:** a large depression in the earth caused by the collapse of a volcano's center.

**geologist:** a scientist who studies rocks, minerals, and the structure of the earth.

# MAKE YOUR OWN
## Rainforest Vine

**1** Draw a leaf template and use it to cut out several pairs of leaves from different shades of green or brown construction paper.

**2** Draw a flower template and cut out several pairs of flowers from colorful construction paper. Flowers like orchids, purple African violets, and the rosy periwinkle are common in African rainforests. Check out some websites for pictures of these plants.

## SUPPLIES

- pencil
- construction paper
- scissors
- long string
- glue
- felt scraps
- markers, glitter, crayons

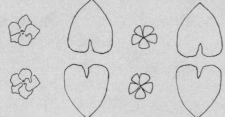

**3** Lay out the pairs of flowers and leaves in two long lines on your work surface. One of each pair should be in each line and the matching pairs should be across from each other in the lines.

**4** Cut a piece of string or yarn that is long enough to stretch across the entire line of construction paper leaves and flowers.

**5** Spread glue on each of the flowers and leaves in one line on your work surface. Lay the string across the glued construction paper figures. Then press the matching flower or leaf on top of its mate like a sandwich.

**6** When the glue is dry, decorate the leaves and flowers on your rainforest vine with pieces of felt, markers, and glitter. You can also cut out rainforest animals like frogs and snakes to add to your rainforest vine.

Plants of the Rainforest   http://www.srl.caltech.edu/personnel/krubal/rainforest/Edit560s6/www/plants.html
The Living Rainforest   http://www.livingrainforest.org/about/plants/rosyperiwinkle
Photos of African violets   http://www.theplantexpert.com/africanviolets/Photos.html

### Chapter 2

# MINERALS

**T**he ancient rocks of Africa hold some of the world's greatest treasures. Gold, iron, copper, platinum, diamonds, and other precious gems lie hidden in the earth in almost every country on the African continent. More than half of all the gold ever mined comes from Africa. Half of the world's glittering diamonds come from South African mines. Sometimes a blessing, sometimes a curse, **minerals** have been a part of African life for thousands of years.

Usually found in the ground, metals such as copper and gold are formed over long periods of time by the heat and pressure of the earth. Most metals are found in rocks called **ore**. By heating the rocks in a process called **smelting**, the metal can be melted from the rock. Once separated, the metal can be shaped, joined, sharpened, and decorated. Metals are shiny and can **conduct** electricity.

## WORDS TO KNOW

**minerals:** substances in rocks and in the ground.

**ore:** a metal-bearing rock.

**smelting:** to melt ore to separate the metal from a rock.

**conduct:** to serve as a channel for heat or electricity.

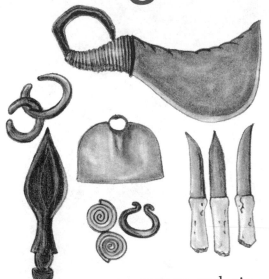

Beginning around 8,000 years ago, early Africans used metals to make stronger weapons, tools, and other objects. Metal spear and arrow tips didn't break. Iron hoes worked better in the fields. Metal made knives and daggers stronger and more efficient. Metal jewelry and ornaments decorated the homes of royalty and the wealthy.

Copper was one of the first metals mined and worked in Africa. But copper is soft, so it wasn't the best choice for weapons and tools. African metalworkers solved this problem by combining copper and tin, creating an **alloy** called bronze. Bronze was much stronger, good for tools and weapons.

One of the strongest metals found in Africa is iron. Iron can be sharpened to a much finer edge than copper or bronze. Iron tools did not lose their edges as quickly as stone tools. Stronger, sharper iron tools made life easier for farmers and hunters.

## WORDS TO KNOW

**alloy:** mixture of metals.

**brass:** an alloy of copper and zinc.

**dung:** animal waste.

**tuyeres:** pipes placed into openings in a furnace where air enters.

**slag:** waste material from smelting iron.

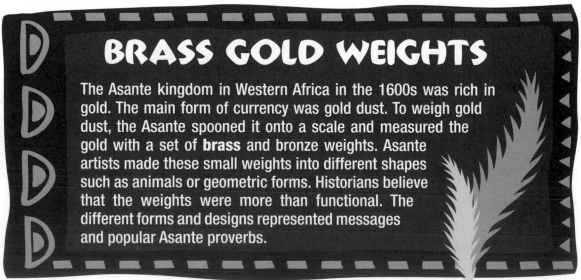

# BRASS GOLD WEIGHTS

The Asante kingdom in Western Africa in the 1600s was rich in gold. The main form of currency was gold dust. To weigh gold dust, the Asante spooned it onto a scale and measured the gold with a set of **brass** and bronze weights. Asante artists made these small weights into different shapes such as animals or geometric forms. Historians believe that the weights were more than functional. The different forms and designs represented messages and popular Asante proverbs.

Unlike copper and gold, iron could not be easily melted from its rocks. Metalworkers had to extract the iron in smelting furnaces. Early iron smelting furnaces were as simple as a bowl dug into the ground. The more complex furnaces had a chimney-like shaft made from clay mixed with **dung** and straw. These furnaces forced air across a hearth and up through the shaft.

### Extracting iron was a complicated process.

To begin the smelting process, the smelter used dry grass to start a fire in the furnace. He layered charcoal on top of the fire. Once the charcoal was hot, the smelter inserted pipes called **tuyeres** and bellows made from goat skins into the sides of the furnace. Then the smelter filled the furnace with more charcoal and added the iron ore. Pumping the bellows forced air through the tuyeres into the furnace. This made the charcoal hotter and better able to release carbon.

As the iron ore absorbed the carbon from the hot charcoal it released oxygen. This caused the iron to separate from the ore. The melting iron then fell below the tuyeres into puddles. The waste material floated to the surface of the puddles and formed into **slag**. Once all the ore had melted and dropped into puddles, the furnace was left to cool. Smelters opened the furnace and raked out pieces of carbonized iron from the slag. This crude iron could now be heated, hammered, and shaped into tools and weapons.

Valuable metals gave objects special meaning. An object made out of copper, brass, bronze, or gold became a symbol of power. The color of metals also sent a message. The reddish tint of copper was a symbol of blood, birth, and death. It attracted good forces and protected against evil.

Iron had a great impact on African daily life. But one of the softest African metals became much more valuable. Unlike other metals used for weapons and tools, gold was valued by the African people for its beauty. Gold was soft, easy to work with, and kept its beautiful, yellowish luster.

In its natural form, gold looks like chunks of golden rock. Smaller amounts can also be found as golden veins running through other rocks. Once heated and melted, it can be poured into molds to form jewelry, vases, and goblets. Only royalty and the wealthy can afford gold.

Ancient Egyptians were one of the first peoples to **mine** gold. Using slaves and prisoners, they dug out gold rocks in Nubia, ground them into a fine powder, and poured the powder into a basin. After adding water to wash away the **sediment**, the gold remained in the basin, ready to heat and craft.

### WORDS TO KNOW

**mine:** to remove minerals from the ground.

**sediment:** tiny bits of material, like dirt.

**elders:** a group of older and wise people in a village.

The Egyptians considered gold to be sacred. Pharaohs covered themselves with gold jewelry. The Egyptians believed that life continued after death in the next world. To help the dead in the afterlife, they would need to bring along items from their current life. Many pharaohs were buried with gold objects to use in the afterlife.

## COPPER COLLARS

Copper collars were common status symbols in Central African societies. The circular collars were cut in the back to allow the wearer to slip them on and off. **Elders** wore copper collars to important meetings. Chiefs gave warriors collars to reward them for courage. Some collars weighed up to 12 pounds (5 kilograms). The larger the collar, the more important the wearer.

Gold, copper, and iron became an important part of African trade. Nicknamed the "Gold Coast," Western Africa supplied European traders with large quantities of gold and other metals. The British named gold coins "guineas" after the Guinea region of West Africa. Tribes that controlled metal sources and mining became wealthy and powerful.

In 1886, Africa experienced one of the world's greatest gold rushes. A gold rush is when a discovery of gold causes a large number of workers to go to the area hoping to find more gold.

**Some South African gold mines are 12,000 feet deep (3,700 meters).**

An Australian gold miner named George Harrison stumbled across a rich gold deposit in the Witwatersrand hills of South Africa, near the city of Johannesburg. Harrison's discovery was in an area of land that was rich in gold. After the discovery, fortune seekers from around the world descended upon Africa. They hoped to get rich panning for gold, just like they had in the California (1848) and Australia (1851) gold rushes.

Panning uses a large metal pan filled with sediment and water. Because gold particles are heavier than the other materials, the gold settles at the bottom of the pan. The miner then shakes the pan back and forth. The sand, gravel, and other sediment washes over the side, leaving the gold. Some miners would build a sluice box to sift out sediment faster than panning. They used shovels and hammers to fill the sluice boxes with sediment for sifting out the surface gold. Either method was inexpensive and easy to do.

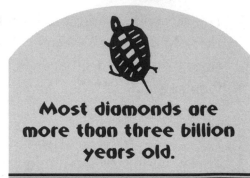

**Most diamonds are more than three billion years old.**

Unfortunately, most of South Africa's gold was encased in rock. Large machinery was needed to extract it from the ground. Mining companies began buying up land and forming large mining corporations. Companies that join together to form one large company can share employees and equipment. These large companies could also pay for the expensive equipment that was needed to extract South African gold. Eventually they grew into the world's largest gold producers.

Only a few years before the Witwatersrand gold rush, diamonds were discovered near the Orange River in South Africa. Diamonds are the hardest natural substance on Earth. Made of pure carbon, they are among the rarest and most valuable gemstones. Some of the most valuable diamonds come from mines in Botswana, Guinea, Angola, Namibia, South Africa, and the Democratic Republic of Congo.

 **Diamonds, like other gemstones, formed deep inside the earth billions of years ago.**

Diamonds started out as pockets of carbon dioxide beneath the earth's crust. Extreme heat and pressure caused the carbon atoms to crystallize into diamonds.

Diamonds could be found in two types of deposits. Some were underground in columns of rocks called pipes that extended up to the surface. Others occurred when volcanoes erupted and brought magma to the earth's surface.

## WORDS TO KNOW

**carat:** the weight of a diamond. One carat equals one-fifth gram.

**prospector:** a person who explores an area for mineral deposits like gold or diamonds.

**civil war:** war between groups in a country.

**blood diamond:** diamond sold to pay for war.

**United Nations:** an international organization that promotes world peace, global cooperation, and human rights.

As the magma cooled into rock, the crystals or gems in the magma were part of the rock. Over time, the rock wore away and these crystals washed into rivers and oceans.

In 1867 a Dutch child playing on the banks of the Orange River found a pretty pebble. A neighbor saw the stone and thought it looked different from other stones in the area. He took the stone to town where it was pronounced to be a yellowish-brown diamond weighing more than 21 **carats**.

Over the next decade, diamond **prospectors** converged on the area. More diamond discoveries were made. People of all nationalities and races dug for diamonds. At first they found diamonds close to the surface. Over time, the diamond seekers had to dig mines deep into the earth. South Africa's richest and most famous diamond mine was named Kimberley after the British Secretary of State, John Wodehouse, 1st Earl of Kimberley.

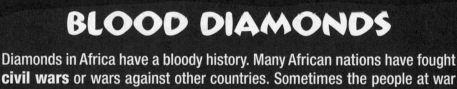

# BLOOD DIAMONDS

Diamonds in Africa have a bloody history. Many African nations have fought **civil wars** or wars against other countries. Sometimes the people at war paid for their guns and weapons by selling their diamonds to other countries. These diamonds became known as conflict or **blood diamonds**.

Blood diamonds came to the world's attention during the brutal civil war in Sierra Leone from 1991 to 2002. The war left many dead or injured. A half million people fled the country. Liberia is a country next to Sierra Leone. The **United Nations** accused the leader of Liberia of giving one side guns and training in exchange for diamonds. Other countries, such as Angola, the Democratic Republic of Congo, the Republic of Congo, and Ivory Coast, have also used blood diamonds to pay for their fighting.

The United Nations has asked buyers not to purchase blood diamonds. How do you know if a diamond is a blood diamond? The United Nations and several South African countries implemented a system in 2003 called the Kimberley Process. Under the Kimberley Process, a diamond receives a certificate of origin. This certifies the diamond is from a conflict-free area. Buyers can ask for a diamond's certificate of origin to make sure they are not helping to pay for a war.

In the early 1870s, a British businessman named Cecil Rhodes wanted to control the area's diamond industry. Over several years, he bought claims and smaller mining companies to eventually form DeBeers Consolidated Mines, Limited. The company was named after the De Beers family farm where many diamonds had been found. Today, the DeBeers name is known for diamonds. It still controls much of the world's diamond production.

**WORDS TO KNOW**

**migrant worker:** a person who moves from place to place to find work.

**refine:** to make pure.

**deforestation:** clearing forests to use the land for other purposes.

The discovery of valuable minerals wasn't always good for the African people. Gold and diamond companies convinced many poor Africans to travel to the mine regions as **migrant workers**. These men labored in the mines in dangerous conditions. Workers faced death or injury from explosions, rock slides, bad air, and flooding.

Mining was also lonely work. Migrant workers spent months away from their families and lived in prison-like dormitories set up by the mining corporations. Black African men labored in the mines, earning small paychecks, while white-owned mining companies grew rich.

Mining also damaged the environment. The chemicals used to **refine** gold, like mercury and cyanide, polluted the land. They seeped into the water, killing plants and animals. Mining was one of the leading causes of **deforestation**. When miners cleared land of all trees and plants, large amounts of sediment clogged the rivers. This killed fish and other wildlife.

Mining chemicals have also been blamed for illnesses in the people living near the mines. These include lead poisoning, cancer, and birth defects.

# MAKE YOUR OWN
## Golden Amulet

Amulets are special charms that are worn or carried to protect its owner. Some amulets were used to protect the wearer against bad spirits. Others were thought to give the wearer extra strength or ability. Think about what you'd like your amulet to represent. Check out some ideas below or use your imagination to create your own.

- Strength – lion
- Wisdom – elephant
- Easy to adapt – crocodile

- Speed – cheetah
- Patience – heart

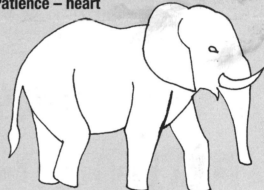

## SUPPLIES

- newspaper or wax paper
- clay
- pencil
- toothpick
- acrylic paint—yellow or golden color
- string
- scissors

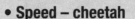

**1** Place a piece of newspaper or wax paper on your work surface. Use the clay to shape your amulet. You can create grooved lines in the amulet using a pencil if you want.

**2** Use the toothpick to poke a small hole near the top of the amulet, so that you will be able to wear it as a necklace.

**3** Put your amulet aside to dry. Once it is fully dried, paint it in a yellowish, golden color to represent precious metal.

**4** Measure the string around your neck. Make it long enough that you'll be able to get your head through the necklace. Cut where you want your amulet necklace to fall.

**5** After the paint is dry, pass the string through the hole in the amulet. Tie the two string ends together and knot it to make sure your necklace doesn't fall apart. Now it's time to get dressed up with your new golden amulet!

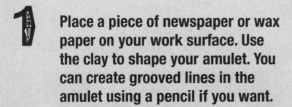

### Chapter 3

# WILDLIFE

**W**ant to see the greatest show on Earth? Come take a **safari** on the African savanna! The sky seems huge as you stand surrounded by rolling grassland in every direction. Flat-topped acacia trees grow scattered among the grasses. This is the Africa you've probably seen in movies and photos.

The savanna is teeming with life. The animals are hard to miss—some of the largest mammals on earth roam the savanna. Lions, elephants, and giraffes all have a role in the savanna's circle of life.

Life on the savanna begins with grass. Enormous herds of **wildebeest**, zebra, and gazelle munch on the grass. As they roam searching for new grasses, the animals fertilize the soil with their droppings, paving the way for new grass to grow.

**WORDS TO KNOW**

**safari:** a journey to explore, most often used to describe a trip to explore Africa.

**wildebeest:** a member of the antelope family that lives in the grassy plains and open woodlands of central, eastern, and southern Africa.

Not everyone on the savanna eats grass, however. It is also home to many **predators**. With so many zebras and gazelles to choose from, hungry **carnivores** like lions and hyenas don't usually miss a meal. Even vultures fly in to grab a bite to eat.

# The Big Five

The most magnificent animals roaming the savanna are known as the Big Five: lion, buffalo, elephant, leopard, and rhinoceros. European hunters who came to Africa in the 1800s called these animals the Big Five. They were the most dangerous, and therefore the most **prestigious**, to hunt. After posing for pictures with their kills, hunters would take a stuffed head or a thick fur back home as a trophy. Today safari hunting is with a camera instead of a gun!

## Lions

The king of Africa is the lion. He rules alone on top of the savanna's pyramid of life, fearing no predator. During the day, a **pride** of lions may sleep 20 hours a day. You'll find them resting under a shady tree or dozing in the tall grass near a herd of antelope.

The pride may have several adult males and even more females and cubs. As the adults doze, the cubs play games. Wrestling and stalking each other's tails, the cubs learn skills that will help them hunt **prey** as adults.

As dusk settles over the savanna, the pride begins to stir, stretching and rubbing against each other. A male shakes his mane and roars, a sound that can be heard almost 5 miles away.

**WORDS TO KNOW**

**predator:** an animal that hunts other animals for food.

**carnivore:** an animal that eats meat.

**prestigious:** held in high regard.

**pride:** group of lions.

**prey:** an animal hunted for food.

The lion's roar signals "here I am" to pride members who may be separated from the group. It also warns other lions to keep away.

Now, it's time to hunt. The female lionesses do most of the hunting for the pride. Working together, they approach an unsuspecting herd of zebra or wildebeest. Because many animals

**Africa's savannas support up to 200 times more animal life than its rainforests.**

can outrun them over long distances, lions sneak up on their prey and launch a surprise attack. Often, one or two lionesses will rush the prey, driving them into an ambush and the waiting jaws of the other lions.

# THE GREAT MIGRATION

Want to see something incredible? Every year, over two million wildebeest, zebra, and gazelle travel between Tanzania's Serengeti National Park and Kenya's Maasai Mara Reserve. They are all in search of grass and water. The timing of the run depends on the season's rain patterns.

On the savanna, there are alternating rainy and dry seasons. The rainy season builds up fresh grass to feed the grazing animals. It usually runs from the end of March into May. Once the rains stop, the plains become hard and dry and the Serengeti's grass is depleted. The animals move north in columns that stretch for miles in search of water and fresh grass. Along the way, predators like lions, hyenas, and leopards follow the herds to grab the occasional unlucky animal. River crossings are perilous as hungry crocodiles lie in wait.

The group arrives at the Maasai Mara Reserve in August or September. They will graze there until the Masai's grass is depleted and the rains return in the south to grow fresh grass. Around November, a shorter, second rainy season replenishes the grass on the Serengeti. Millions of animals surge southward again, hungry for the fresh grass. When they return to the Serengeti, the migration circle is complete. In their own amazing way, the herds of the Serengeti efficiently use their resources and support nature's cycles of growth and renewal.

## Cape Buffalo

One of the biggest, meanest beasts on the savanna is the Cape Buffalo. Some people believe it rivals the hippopotamus as the most dangerous animal in Africa. It's hard to imagine that a relative of the domestic cow can be very dangerous. But an angry buffalo charges at 30 miles an hour, brandishing its thick, sharp horns. It's easy to understand why you don't want to anger one.

The buffalo's huge horns curve like handlebars from its head. Their sharp tips can easily gore an attacker. This huge animal can be more than 5 feet tall (1.5 meters). Its thick, stocky body can weigh as much as 1,300 pounds (590 kilograms) That's half as heavy as a Honda Civic! Because of their size, Cape Buffalo don't have to worry about many predators, other than lions.

**No two giraffes have the same pattern of spots and no two zebras have the same pattern of stripes.**

Buffalo herds gather near rivers, creeks, and water holes. Because buffalo don't sweat much, they need to cool off in the water or mud under the hot African sun. Like the cow, the buffalo doesn't hunt for food—it grazes on the savanna's grass.

## Elephants

What is the biggest animal on the savanna? The answer is easy. The world's largest land animal, adult elephants can stand 12 feet tall (3.6 meters) at their shoulders and weigh more than six tons (5.4 metric tons). That's more than your average family minivan! Even their teeth are big—an elephant's tusk is actually an incisor tooth.

Along with all that brawn, elephants also have brains. Have you ever heard someone say "I have a memory like an elephant?"

That's because elephants really can remember places, other animals, and events for a long, long time. This helps them survive on the African plains because they are able to remember all the good places to find food and water. Smart elephants also use tools. They'll use a stick to scratch an itch, or move a log under a tree to use as a stepping stool to reach a yummy piece of fruit.

**Four of the five fastest land animals on earth live in Africa. The cheetah is the fastest at 70 miles (112.6 kilometers) per hour, with the wildebeest, lion, and Thomson's gazelle close behind.**

Elephants even have a language of their own. They use more than 70 different sounds, including trumpets, squeals, screams, roars, and rumbles. Some rumbles mean "let's go in this direction." Others sounds are used to contact distant family members.

**The tip of the African elephant's trunk is so coordinated that it can turn the pages of a book.**

If you are a young elephant, you'd better listen to your mom. She's the boss. That's because elephants live in **matriarchal** families led by the oldest female. Female elephants develop close family bonds and may stay with the herd for their entire

**WORDS TO KNOW**

**matriarchal:** group headed by a female leader.

lives. Male elephants strike out on their own when they're about 14, hanging out with other males until they are strong enough to compete for females.

Elephant families are a tight-knit bunch. Mothers caress their babies with their trunks. They also intertwine their trunks to greet each other, like a handshake. If one elephant gets injured, the others will try to help out. The family will even mourn when one dies, staying with the body for a few days and covering it with branches.

## Leopards

Who is one of the sneakiest animals on the savanna? At night, the leopard stalks its prey, such as an unsuspecting antelope or zebra. The leopard then rushes in and pulls the animal to the ground with his claws. One bite on the throat usually kills the prey on the spot.

But the leopard's work is not done yet. He uses his powerful jaws to drag his meal away. The leopard does this to enjoy his dinner in a more private place, away from the hyenas and vultures who might want to join him. These animals, known as scavengers, will eat animals killed by other predators. The leopard is so strong that it can even drag his kill up into the branches of a tree. There, resting on a branch, it eats.

If a leopard could talk, it might say "just leave me alone!" They prefer to live by themselves, even walking away from other leopards they meet on the savanna. A leopard marks his territory by clawing bark, rubbing his fur on a tree, or spraying urine. This warns others to stay away.

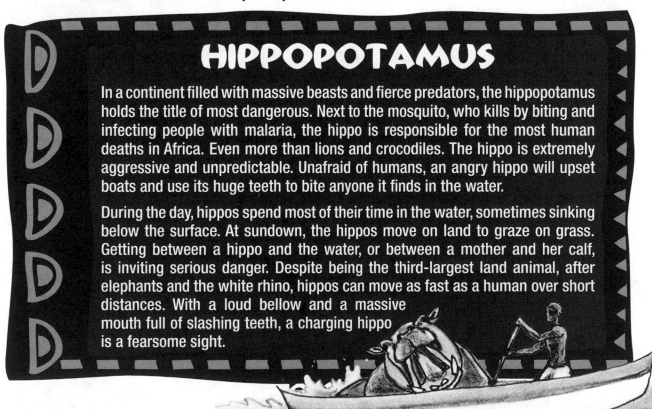

## HIPPOPOTAMUS

In a continent filled with massive beasts and fierce predators, the hippopotamus holds the title of most dangerous. Next to the mosquito, who kills by biting and infecting people with malaria, the hippo is responsible for the most human deaths in Africa. Even more than lions and crocodiles. The hippo is extremely aggressive and unpredictable. Unafraid of humans, an angry hippo will upset boats and use its huge teeth to bite anyone it finds in the water.

During the day, hippos spend most of their time in the water, sometimes sinking below the surface. At sundown, the hippos move on land to graze on grass. Getting between a hippo and the water, or between a mother and her calf, is inviting serious danger. Despite being the third-largest land animal, after elephants and the white rhino, hippos can move as fast as a human over short distances. With a loud bellow and a massive mouth full of slashing teeth, a charging hippo is a fearsome sight.

When not hunting, leopards like to lounge in trees, draped on a branch with paws and tail dangling in the air. Because leopards are so sneaky, they can live close to villages without being noticed. Village livestock are tempting targets. The leopard may decide to steal a goat or two for lunch.

**keratin:** a tough protein substance found in hair, fingernails, horns, and hooves.

**primates:** a grouping of animals that includes apes, monkeys, and humans.

# Rhinos

The rhinoceros has a curving, spear-like horn on its snout and skin up to 2 inches thick. It might be the savanna's version of an army tank. The rhinoceros name means nose horn. Some even have two horns. But did you know that a rhino's horn is not a bone? It is made out of **keratin**, the same substance found in hair, fingernails, and hooves. Just like your fingernails, a rhino's horn keeps growing all the time. If it breaks off, they can grow a new one. Good thing, because a rhino uses its horn to fight off attackers and defend its young.

In Africa there are two types of rhinoceros—the black rhino and the white rhino. Despite their names, neither animal is black or white. They are both grey! The main difference is the shape of their heads. White rhinos have a low-hanging head and a wide, square mouth that's perfect for grazing on grass. Black rhinos have a pointed upper lip, called a prehensile lip. It works like a finger to wrap around the twigs, leaves, and fruit it wants to eat.

The rhino has a reputation for being ill-tempered. They often live alone or in small groups with their young. Rhinos have a great sense of smell and well-developed hearing. They will charge any disturbing smell or sound, thinking it is a threat. Because of their poor eyesight, black rhinos have been known to attack rocks and trees by mistake. Rhinos fight with each other over territory and females. A rhino may look awkward, but in fact, they can thunder along at 30 miles per hour and jump, twist, and turn quickly.

# THREAT OF EXTINCTION

For a variety of reasons, many animal habitats are rapidly disappearing. Clearing forest for farms and houses, logging wood for money, and overgrazing cattle on the savanna contribute to the problem. The search for diamonds and metals has destroyed many habitats. Central Africa's mountain gorilla is one of the most endangered **primates** in the world due to the vanishing rainforest.

Hunting has endangered many animals. When European explorers arrived in Africa, they were amazed by the spectacular animals. People who liked the thrill of adventure and hunting packed their bags for Africa. Hunters wanted to bring home animal skins, stuffed trophy heads, or valuable tusks. Others wanted to capture the animals and send them to zoos and carnivals. Thousands of zebras, leopards, elephants, lions, and other animals were killed. The black rhinoceros was almost completely wiped out.

Today, hunting is strictly controlled. Many wildlife parks hire guards to patrol the land and look for poachers, who still hunt against the law. They usually want to sell the animals or animal parts, like elephant tusks, for money. In some countries, like Tanzania, convicted poachers face 15 to 50 years in jail. Poaching penalties in other countries may be more of a slap on the wrist.

Many scientists, conservationists, and African communities are working to protect African animals and their habitats. Large game reserves provide a safe place for wildlife to thrive and increase their numbers.
Let's hope it isn't too late.

# Wildlife Diversity

While the Big Five are some of the most popular animals in Africa, there are thousands of other species on the continent. Wildebeest, giraffes, and cheetahs also roam the grassy plains. Fierce hippos and crocodiles lurk in rivers. Gorillas and other rare primates make their home in the rainforests. Altogether, more than 1,100 species of mammals, 2,000 bird species, and hundreds of reptiles, amphibians, and fish live in Africa. This makes it one of the world's most spectacular places for wildlife.

# MAKE YOUR OWN
## African savanna

## SUPPLIES

- newspaper
- modeling clay
- paint and markers
- green and blue construction paper
- scissors
- glue
- large piece of cardboard

**1** Spread newspaper over your work surface. Use the clay to form several animals you would find on the African savanna. Make groups of giraffe, lions, elephants, zebra, and wildebeest. You can also use your clay to form one or two acacia trees.

**2** After the clay has dried and hardened, color the animals with paint and markers. Make golden lions, spotted giraffe, and striped zebra. Paint works well for the overall base colors while markers are good to add smaller details. Cut and glue green construction paper leaves to the tops of your trees.

**3** Now prepare your savanna by covering one side of the cardboard with green construction paper. Glue the paper in place. This represents the fertile grasses of the savanna plains. Next, cut a piece of blue construction paper that will be a source of water for your savanna animals. You can choose to make a small watering hole, a larger lake, or a meandering river. Glue the water in place on your savanna.

**4** Arrange your animals on the savanna as you might find them in Africa. Groups of zebra and elephant roam together, maybe drinking water. Lions lounge beneath trees to escape the hot daytime sun, but may lurk near a herd of prey. Giraffe nibble at the top of an acacia tree. Have fun setting up your own savanna world!

# MAKE YOUR OWN
## Leopard Mask

## SUPPLIES

- newspaper
- stiff cardstock
- pencil
- scissors
- orange and brown paint and paintbrush
- brown and black construction paper
- glue
- hole punch
- string

**1** Place a piece of newspaper on your work surface. Draw the outline of your leopard mask on the cardstock. Cut out the mask and eyeholes.

**2** Paint the front of the mask with the orange paint. After the orange coat has dried, add the leopard's spots with brown paint. Outline the eyeholes with brown paint.

**3** Cut out thin strips of black construction paper for whiskers. Using the brown construction paper, cut out an oval-shaped nose and two half-circle shapes to fit inside the ears.

**4** Once the paint on your mask has dried, glue the ears and nose onto your leopard. Glue the whiskers on the sides of the nose.

**5** Using the hole punch, make two holes on either side of the mask. Tie a piece of string to each hole. Then tie the two ends of the string behind your head to secure the mask on your face. It's time to roar!

**Variation:** You can substitute orange construction paper for the main mask and use markers to color the leopard's spots.

### chapter 4

# GREAT CIVILIZATIONS

**S**ome ancient African civilizations were as magnificent as any in the world. Many of these great kingdoms flourished in areas rich with fertile soil and vast amounts of gold. Others controlled trade to become wealthy and powerful. These African civilizations were sophisticated, with complex systems of government. People traded goods and services. Skilled craftsmen produced amazing pieces of art and **architecture**. These ancient societies left rich contributions to Africa's history.

## Ancient Egypt

Ancient Egypt was one of the most powerful civilizations of all time. It existed from around 3100 **BCE** to 639 **CE**. Its territory stretched across Northern Africa from the Mediterranean Sea to today's country of Sudan. Egypt's power came from its vast natural resources.

The Nile River was the most important of these resources. When the mighty Nile flooded its banks each year, it left a fertile soil behind. The Egyptians became self-sufficient with a constant supply of food. They kept animals like cattle and grew barley, vegetables, and fruit.

South of Egypt in modern-day Sudan, the Nubian desert gave Egypt immense gold mines. This gold was a source of great wealth and the real power of the Egyptian rulers.

**WORDS TO KNOW**

**architecture:** the art and science of designing and constructing buildings.

**BCE/CE:** Before Common Era, leading up to the year 0, and Common Era, after 0.

**pharaoh:** an ancient Egyptian king.

**pyramids:** monuments that hold the tombs of ancient Egyptian pharaohs.

Ancient Egypt was home to many of the world's most skilled artists and builders. Egyptian **pharaohs** hired them to create beautiful jewelry, pottery, glass beads, and other prized art pieces. Egyptian architects designed magnificent temples to honor the gods. They built the **pyramids**, where the pharaohs and their families were buried.

# HATSHEPSUT

Princess Hatshepsut was born into Egypt's royal family in the fifteenth century BCE. When her husband died as a young man, she stepped in to rule until her 5-year-old stepson was old enough to be crowned pharaoh.

Hatshepsut did a pharaoh's daily work. She met with government officials, made laws, and took part in religious ceremonies. Over the years, her powers grew. After 7 years, Hatshepsut crowned herself pharaoh, King Hatshepsut. She chose to wear the traditional pharaoh's clothing—even a false beard on her chin. Many people believe Hatshepsut dressed as a man to show the Egyptian gods and people she was the rightful pharaoh.

Hatshepsut was a peaceful ruler. She ordered the building of hundreds of shrines, monuments, and statues. She also sent out exploring expeditions. King Hatshepsut ruled Egypt for 20 years, until her death.

Ancient Egypt's king was called a pharaoh. Ancient Egyptians believed that their king was the son of the god Amun-Ra. The pharaoh owned all the land in Egypt.

Egyptians believed in the spirit world after death. They took great care when burying their dead, preserving bodies as mummies. First they removed the heart and other organs. Then they stuffed the body with linen, straw, or sawdust, and wrapped the body with strips of linen cloths. The mummified body was placed in a coffin or a huge stone box called a sarcophagus and buried in a tomb. Pharaohs and their wives were buried in pyramid tombs filled with food, drink, and personal items needed in their spirit life.

Ancient Egypt developed one of the world's oldest and most interesting methods of writing, called **hieroglyphics**. Hieroglyphics were pictures and symbols that represented words or sounds. Very few Egyptians could read or write. **Scribes** copied texts, wrote letters, recorded court decisions, and kept track of accounts. They began training around age 10.

**hieroglyphics:** ancient Egypt's earliest form of writing.

**scribes:** ancient Egyptians who read and wrote hieroglyphs.

# The Great Zimbabwe

The Great Zimbabwe kingdom emerged a thousand years ago from ancestors of the Shona people. This ethnic group in modern day Zimbabwe, Zambia, and Mozambique spoke a similar language. The kingdom thrived in the Zambezi Valley of south central Africa. Unlike most African kingdoms, which rose near the coast, Great Zimbabwe developed inland.

The power and wealth of these farmers and cattle keepers grew when Arab traders arrived on the East African coast. Evidence suggests the Great Zimbabwe bought gold from miners and sold it to these traders.

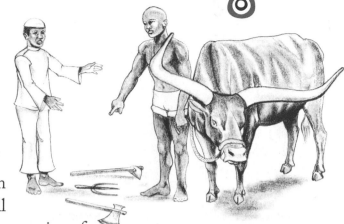

They traded goods like hoes and axes to farmers and miners in return for copper, cattle, and other goods.

The name Zimbabwe comes from the Shona word meaning "stone buildings." Their city was a system of massive stone walls, with three main areas. Archaeologists believe the Hill Complex was used as a temple. It was a series of enclosures linked by stone passageways. The Valley Complex probably housed the city's elite citizens, who would have lived in huts sheltered by the walls.

## The Great Enclosure was where the king lived.

Builders constructed the magnificent walls of Great Zimbabwe from granite rocks found in the surrounding hills. After splitting the rocks into even slabs, they lay the stones one on top of the other. Each layer sloped slightly inward to stabilize the wall. The Great Zimbabwean builders became highly skilled at dry stonewalling—creating walls without mortar or cement. They built the highest dry walls in Africa.

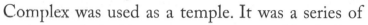

One of the city's most impressive stone monuments was the *Imba Huru*, or the Great Enclosure. Sitting on top of a plateau, it had an amazing view of the surrounding grasslands. The Great Enclosure's main oval wall stood about 32 feet (9.7 meters) high and ran 800 feet (244 meters) long. Inside stood more massive walls. Historians believe the walls took over 400 years to build and portions of it remain standing today.

By 1450, the people abandoned the city. Over-farming may have stripped the land and it could no longer support so many people. Others think the kingdom declined because trade routes shifted to other areas.

# Kingdom of Benin

Five hundred years ago, the Kingdom of Benin glittered on the west coast of Africa along the Atlantic Ocean. One famous **oba** of Benin was named Ewuare. Ewuare conquered many neighboring villages. He established a government and appointed local chiefs to represent areas of Benin. These local chiefs collected **tributes** of palm oil, yams, and other foods on behalf of the oba. Paying tributes to the oba was like paying taxes today. Ewuare also introduced the idea that the oba title should pass from father to son.

The Benin obas supported the arts. Metalworkers created incredible pieces of bronze and brass art like sculptures, amulets, and plaques. Almost all of Benin's art was created to honor the obas. On the palace walls, the obas hung brass scenes of palace life and the Benin kingdom's history. The obas also wore intricate and detailed brass jewelry for royal ceremonies.

**The Kingdom of Benin was located in today's Nigeria, not the modern-day country of Benin.**

Benin traded ivory, palm oil, and pepper with other African kingdoms, as well as with Dutch and Portuguese traders. Bronze statues, carved masks, and fabrics became popular trade goods as well. Benin also participated in the slave trade with other African kingdoms. Unlike some African kingdoms, however, the Benin did not trade slaves with the Europeans.

In the late 1800s, the British conquered the Kingdom of Benin. The British burned the city and destroyed many pieces of art. Eventually the Benin people gained their independence, becoming the modern country of Nigeria in 1960.

## WORDS TO KNOW

**oba:** king of the ancient Benin civilization.

**tribute:** payment made by one ruler or state to another as a sign of submission.

**kente cloth:** a type of fabric made of interwoven cloth strips.

# The Asante Empire

From the late 1600s, the Asante ruled in West Africa near today's southern Ghana. The Asante kingdom grew wealthy trading gold and slaves to Europeans or other African groups. War captives were enslaved or conquered groups paid tribute in the form of people. In return for slaves, the Asante received guns and other European goods. The guns helped them grow even stronger.

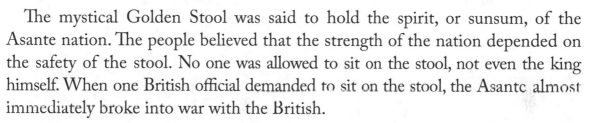

The Asante king had many chiefs below him to help run the kingdom. He lived in a wealthy household surrounded by gold and brass artwork, wood carvings, and furniture. Weavers also created brightly colored woven **kente cloth**.

The mystical Golden Stool was said to hold the spirit, or sunsum, of the Asante nation. The people believed that the strength of the nation depended on the safety of the stool. No one was allowed to sit on the stool, not even the king himself. When one British official demanded to sit on the stool, the Asante almost immediately broke into war with the British.

Even though the Asante strongly resisted, the British took control of their gold and slave trade on the West African coast in the early 1900s. The Asante remained a colony of the British Empire until Ghana's independence in 1957.

## ADINKRA PRINTING

According to Asante legend, Adinkra printing originated when a rival king named Adinkra was captured. To express his sorrow, he wore cloth printed with geometric patterns. Asante artists began using the designs in their own cloth. Royal craftsmen drew grid lines on the cloth and filled each square with different stamped designs. Most squares had one stamp repeated several times. The stamps usually had a special meaning. Some examples include a wooden comb (beauty and love), watery shrub (purity and cleanliness), hen's feet (parental discipline and care), and a palm tree (self sufficiency and wealth). The color of the cloth was important as well. Red, brown, and black were used for funerals and mourning. White cloths were used for celebrations.

# MAKE YOUR OWN
## Adinkra stamping

To make adinkra cloth, artists put dye on patterned blocks made from boiled tree bark, but you can use potatoes instead.

**NOTE: This activity uses a knife so you may want to ask an adult for help.**

## SUPPLIES

- newspaper
- permanent felt-tip marker
- ruler
- several pieces of plain white paper
- knife
- two or three firm potatoes
- paper towels
- stamp pad and ink

**1** Cover your work surface with newspaper. Use a ruler and permanent marker to draw lines on your plain white paper. Make the lines up and down and then across to form several squares on your paper.

**2** Carefully cut a ¾-inch-thick slice (2 centimeters) from the potato. Trim the edges of the potato slice to make it square. You can also make a cross-shaped stamp by cutting away the four corners of your slice. Dry the potato slice with a paper towel.

**3** Press the potato stamp onto the ink pad. Make sure the pad is well-inked! Add extra ink if you need it. Press the potato stamp inside one of the squares on your paper. Repeat the stamp several times within the same square.

**4** Use more potato slices to create more stamps with different geometric patterns. Some stamps may be stars, squares, V's, or anything else you can think of. You can also rotate your stamps to use them in different ways on the paper.

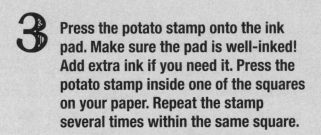

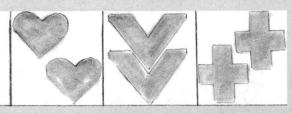

**Variation:** Use adinkra stamping to make your own cards. Decorate T-shirts using fabric paint instead of a stamp pad.

### chapter 5

# HUNTERS, HERDERS & FARMERS

**W**hat would you eat if there were no grocery stores? In Africa, many people live in areas without a central food store. These people find food in ways that are centuries old. Some, such as the Mbuti men and women, hunt and gather food in the Congo rainforest. Others, like the Samburu in Kenya, tend after **herds** of cattle. Still others farm in order to eat and to produce goods to trade.

## Hunters and Gatherers

Before farming and herding, the earliest people in Africa hunted and gathered food to survive. The men were the hunters. To be successful, the hunter studied the habits of his prey by observing their behavior.

## WORDS TO KNOW

**herd:** gather, keep, or drive sheep, cattle, or other animals.

**snare:** an animal trap.

**larva:** an insect in its wingless, wormlike stage of life.

**pupae:** an insect in its cocoon where it changes from a larva to an adult.

**chrysomelid:** a small, brightly colored beetle.

**track:** to follow.

Knowing where and when the animals ate, drank, and slept helped the hunter stalk the animal during the hunt. To trap smaller animals, hunters made **snares** of plant fibers or twisted animal gut. For hunting larger animals, a bow and arrow was the hunter's favorite and most effective tool.

The arrow itself did not usually kill the hunter's prey. Instead, the animal died from poison on the arrow. Hunters crafted the arrow's tip from wood, stone, or bone. Then they applied poison made from beetles, plants, or snake venom. One common poison came from the **larva** or **pupae** of **chrysomelid** beetles. To apply the poison, the hunter squeezed the contents of the larva directly onto the arrow. He could also mix the squeezed contents of the larva with spit and plant juice, which acted as an adhesive. He would then apply the mixture to the arrow.

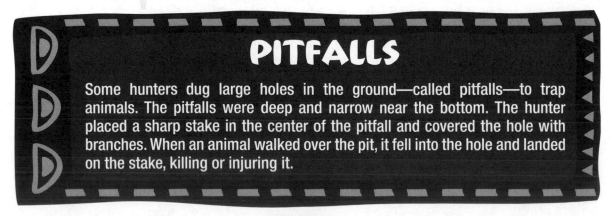

## PITFALLS

Some hunters dug large holes in the ground—called pitfalls—to trap animals. The pitfalls were deep and narrow near the bottom. The hunter placed a sharp stake in the center of the pitfall and covered the hole with branches. When an animal walked over the pit, it fell into the hole and landed on the stake, killing or injuring it.

The poison was very potent. Hunters had to be careful not to poison themselves by accident. They would smear poison just below the arrow's tip because they didn't want to risk pricking themselves with the poisonous tip. Others wore special wrist guards so the arrow wouldn't nick their wrists as they shot it from the bow. To kill his prey, the hunter only had to graze it with the arrow because the poison was so deadly.

The poison did not kill the animal immediately. It could take several hours for the animal to collapse and die. For the largest animals, like a giraffe or elephant, it might be a few days. During this time, the hunter **tracked** the wounded animal.

---

**Hunters know what time of day an animal passed through an area by looking at its hoof prints underneath a tree. If the tracks are under the west side of the tree, the animal escaped the hot African sun by standing in the morning shade. Tracks under the east side means the animal stood there in the afternoon. If the tracks are in the open, the animal may have slept there at night.**

---

Tracking was an important skill for hunters. They could follow animals from the faintest marks in the sand or dirt. Trackers learned all sorts of information from an animal's hoof print. They could tell what type of animal it was, how fast it was going, if it was alone, and even what it had been eating. If the hoof prints were uneven and different depths, the hunter knew that the animal was wounded. By looking at how deep the print was, how much wind there was, and if any grass and twigs had fallen into the hoof print, the hunter could glean how many minutes or hours had gone by since the animal made the print.

When a hunter caught and killed an animal, every part of it would be used. Families ate the animal's meat after the hunter cut away the section where the arrow struck the animal. The poison damaged the animal's heart but did not spread throughout the body, leaving most of the meat safe to eat. From the animal's bones, hunters created tools, like arrow heads. Animal skins and furs became clothing, shelter, bags, and slings.

Meanwhile, the women would gather food. They had to know the land and the growing cycles of plants—just like the hunters knew their animal prey's habits. The women would collect wild fruits, melons, and nuts. With large digging sticks, they dug up edible roots from the ground. They also captured insects like termites, caterpillars, and locusts, which were a good source of protein. Gathering food was more reliable than hunting. Many times, a hunter would return without a kill. Gatherers almost always returned with something to eat.

# BUSHMAN'S BOW & ARROW

The Bushmen are an ethnic group in southern Africa. Their hunting bows are made from tough wood and measure 2 to 3 feet (1 meter) long. The middle part of the bow is about 1 inch thick (2.5 centimeters), tapering towards the ends. To make the bow, the hunter first picks a straight branch and strips it of bark, twigs, and leaves. He bends the branch and ties it against a pole to dry. Then he shaves the branch with a stone or knife until he is happy with the thickness. The hunter may rub grease on the wood to prevent it from cracking or splitting.

Arrows generally have stone or bone tips, but some are made from iron. The tip and its collar are connected to the arrow's shaft through a bone or wood link. When the hunter shoots an animal with his arrow, the impact causes the link to splinter the main shaft. The shaft falls away, leaving the point stuck in the animal. If the point carries poison, it spreads into the animal's body.

Hunters and gatherers usually lived in small, family-sized groups. They didn't build permanent homes because they needed to be able to move quickly to follow animal movements and plant harvests. Instead, they used caves or overhanging rocks for shelter, or made temporary shelters from branches, grass, and stones.

Every person had a role in finding food for the group. Even children gathered food. This made for some of the most equal societies in Africa. While most African people no longer hunt and gather food, some ethnic groups like the San in southern Africa still follow this traditional way of life.

**WORDS TO KNOW**

**sorghum:** a type of grain grass common in Africa.

**drought:** a long period of extremely dry weather.

# Farming for Food

Grains like wheat, barley, **sorghum,** and millet grow wild across Africa. Over time, gatherers realized they could grow these plants themselves. They learned that leaving the best seeds behind grew better crops the next year. Weeding helped the crops grow strong and healthy. Even better, hoeing and plowing loosened the soil, made weeding easier.

Farming had a big impact on the way people lived in Africa. Since farmers didn't need to constantly move in search of food, they could settle in a fertile place and grow their food nearby. Farmers could build more permanent houses and keep more personal items, like tools and pottery. Many homes included storage areas for these items.

African farmers also grow imported crops, like bananas from Asia and cassava and maize from America.

Farming was also a more reliable way to produce a lot of food. When crops were abundant, farmers could store extra food. This came in handy during times of **drought**. As a result, families grew bigger.

# A KIKUYU LEGEND

The Kikuyu are an ethnic group from East Africa. According to Kikuyu legend, an old man who lay dying sent his three sons into the world. He gave each a gift to help them get started in their new life. The first son received an arrow for hunting, and his people became the Dorobo. The second son received a hoe for farming—his people became the Kikuyu ethnic group. The third son received a stick. He used the stick to herd cattle and his family became the Maasai.

For hunters and gatherers, children were a burden to bring along when they had to be on the move. This helped keep their families small. Children could help with farming chores, however. More children meant more helpers!

Communities grew larger. Since not everyone in the community had to work to produce food, some people became craftsmen. Others became religious or community leaders. These people traded their skills or goods for food.

Being a farmer had its problems as well. As people took different jobs, some became richer than others. People were no longer equals. Also, farmers depended on the soil and rain for their crops to grow. If drought or floods ruined their crops, farmers could find themselves without food.

# The Herding Life

Some people in Africa survived by herding livestock, such as cattle, sheep, and goats. Herders learned to control the movement of wild animals. Since they used long sticks to drive the animals in the direction they wanted, herders were called the people of the stick. The herders had to protect their animals from predators.

Like the farmer, the herder's life depended on the climate and environment. Rain meant more grass and a larger herd. When rain was scarce some of the animals died. Herders had to move with their livestock in search of grassy pastures, so they usually had less permanent homes than farmers.

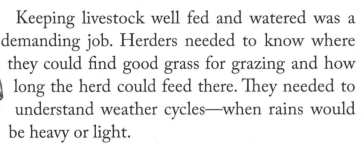

Keeping livestock well fed and watered was a demanding job. Herders needed to know where they could find good grass for grazing and how long the herd could feed there. They needed to understand weather cycles—when rains would be heavy or light.

For herders who did this well, the result was a large, healthy herd—a sign of wealth. The animals of the herd were valuable because they converted the grass they ate into milk, a renewable source of nutrients. A large herd also protected a herder during a drought because he was more likely to have some of his herd survive.

Most herders did not eat the cattle meat. Sometimes, on special occasions or when food was scarce, a herder killed for food. But most of the time, herders drank the herd's milk. They also traded cattle with farmers for other goods.

In Africa today, herders are a small percentage of the population. Some people combine herding and farming to make a living. Others, like the Samburu of Kenya and the Dinka of Sudan, continue the herding way of life.

**In some communities, a herder will give valuable cattle to his bride's family for a dowry.**

# GOATS AND SHEEP

Cattle were found wild in Africa, but goats and sheep were probably imported from the Middle East and adopted by African herders. Goats are important because they can survive with less food and water than other livestock, such as cattle and sheep. When a drought dries up the rain, animals will stop producing milk. In these conditions, a goat is the last to stop giving milk. When the rains finally return, the goats make milk again quickly.

# MAKE YOUR OWN
## Horned staff

In this project, you'll make a staff with horns to represent the importance of cattle in Africa.

## SUPPLIES

- wooden yardstick, dowel, or thin cardboard tube
- construction paper
- tape
- paint, markers, other decorative items
- pencil
- paper
- cardboard or stiff cardstock
- scissors
- glue

**2** Next, design your power symbol. You might want to practice your design on regular paper. Also add two horns to the top of your symbol to represent the horns of cattle. Once you've finished your design, draw it on your cardboard or cardstock.

**3** Then you can cut out your power symbol. Color it with markers or paint. You can also use items such as buttons or craft jewels to decorate your symbol.

**4** Using glue or tape, attach your power symbol to the top of your staff.

**1** Cover the wooden yardstick or dowel with construction paper. This will be your base to decorate your staff. Decorate your staff with markers, paint, buttons, craft jewels, beads, seeds, and other items. You may want to look up pattern ideas from certain African areas and groups of people. Add as much pattern and decoration to the staff as you want!

# MAKE YOUR OWN
## Dogon Antelope Mask

Many African ethnic groups, like the Dogon, perform rituals and ceremonies to ensure a successful harvest. For the Dogon, the antelope is a symbol of a hardworking farmer. Antelope masks are often a rectangular shape with horns at the top. Dancers wearing the masks use sticks to hit the ground to represent both the antelope's pawing and the hoeing of farmers.

## SUPPLIES

- poster board or other stiff cardstock, about 24 inches by 24 inches (61 by 61 centimeters)
- pencil
- scissors
- paint and brushes
- hole punch
- string

**1** Fold the poster board in half. Pretend the folded edge is the center of your mask. Using a pencil, draw the outline of half of your mask on one side of the folded poster board.

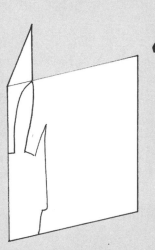

**2** Carefully cut out your mask, cutting through both layers of poster board. Draw rectangular eyeholes on the mask and cut them out.

**3** Paint the mask a base color. Much of Dogon artwork uses red, black, and white colors. Once the base is dry, decorate your mask as you wish. You can experiment with different colors and designs.

**4** Use the hole punch to make hole on each side of the mask right above ear-level. Tie a piece of string in each hole and try on your mask!

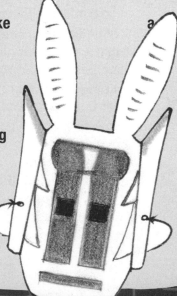

# MAKE YOUR OWN
## Senufo Mud Painting

The Senufo people live in Cote d'Ivoire in West Africa. Senufo hunters wear clothes decorated with mud paintings. They use animal images because they believe the spirits of these animals will protect the hunters from injury and bring about a successful hunt. To make a black paint, Senufo artists collect mud. They also boil leaves to make a liquid dye. The artist dips a knife into the liquid dye and draws outlines of animals and other designs. After the outline dries, the artist uses the thick mud paint to fill in parts of the outlines. You can make a mud-painted T-shirt for yourself. Cover your work surface with newspaper. This can get messy!

## SUPPLIES

- newspaper
- kitchen strainer
- disposable plastic container
- ½ cup dirt
- water
- plastic spoon
- ½ cup nontoxic acrylic or poster paint—blue or black
- white T-shirt
- pencil & black permanent marker
- toothbrush & small paintbrush

**1** Put the dirt into the strainer set over the plastic container. Slowly run water over the dirt until all the dirt has run through the strainer into the container. Use the spoon to help push the dirt through if you need to. Let the mud sink to the bottom for a few minutes. Carefully pour out the water. Mix the paint into the mud left at the bottom.

**2** Place the T-shirt on the work surface with a layer of newspaper between the front and back of the shirt. This will keep the paint from seeping through to the other side.

**3** Senufo artists often used animals like crocodiles, turtles, monkeys, and lizards in their work. You might want to practice your design on a piece of paper first. When you've finished, draw the design outline in pencil on your T-shirt. Then, go over the pencil outline with a permanent marker.

**4** Using a toothbrush to scoop some of the mud paint, fill in some of your outlines with the paint. Experiment with ways to make striped patterns with the toothbrush. You can use a small paintbrush to fill in smaller areas and also to add decorative lines and dots to your T-shirt.

**5** Let your T-shirt dry overnight. Shake off any excess mud outside. Then, hand wash the shirt in cold water, air dry, and it's ready to wear!

### Chapter 6

# ETHNIC GROUPS

**A**ll across Africa, people belong to **ethnic groups.** Thousands of years ago, ethnic groups formed from families and extended families, called clans. Neighboring clans traded with each other and shared common resources like water and food.

Sometimes called tribes, these groups of people spoke a common language. They developed a common set of rituals. They made rules that told their people what behavior was right and wrong. If anyone broke the rules, the group decided on a fair punishment. Living within an ethnic group can be like living in the same neighborhood with all your aunts, uncles, cousins, and friends.

Most ethnic groups choose a leader. The leader is usually smart and wise, and is good at getting people to work together. Some groups allow their leaders to pass their title down from father to son, like European **monarchies** do.

## WORDS TO KNOW

**ethnic group:** a group with common ancestors sharing customs, languages, and beliefs.

**monarchy:** supreme power held by a single person like a king or queen.

**elders:** wise people in a village.

**gemsbok:** large antelope found in Africa.

Other ethnic groups are led by a group of people, called **elders**. The elders are usually the oldest, wisest people.

Leaders have several important jobs. The leader settles arguments between people with fair judgments. A leader also organizes the group and decides how to divide shared resources, such as food and water. In years past, when fighting among different groups was more common, the leader often led his warriors into battle.

# The San People

One of the oldest and most famous ethnic groups in Africa is the San people. Historians believe the San have lived in southern Africa for almost 30,000 years. The San people had lighter skin than most Africans, a golden

Sharing and treating each other as equals helped the San live peacefully for thousands of years without a war.

yellow to apricot shade. The average man was only 5 feet tall, and women were slightly shorter.

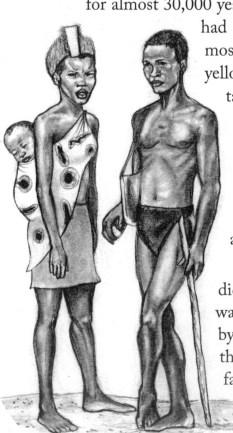

The early San were a hunting and gathering people, living in small clan groups of around 30 members. They lived in temporary homes made of long sticks tied at the top with vines and covered with grass and leaves. These shelters protected them from the wind and were easily built again when the group moved.

Like many hunting and gathering people, the San did not have a group leader. Each person in the clan was equal. Without money or trading, the San survived by sharing with each other. A successful hunter chose the best and biggest portion for his family, then other families shared the rest of the meat.

At night, the clan gathered to dance and sing around the fire. Many dances mimicked animal movements to bring the dancers closer to nature's spirits. Handmade drums provided a beat for the dancers. So did rattles made from large butterfly cocoons filled with pieces of ostrich eggshell. Music came from reed flutes and bells made of leather and stone.

The San told stories. Songs and stories told ancient legends, talked about daily life, and passed down San history. Some songs were used in religious ceremonies, while others were just for fun. Listening to a San story around the fire, you would hear the distinctive clicking and popping sounds as they spoke that are part of the San language.

The San celebrated life as it happened. A child becoming an adult, rains falling, or a good hunt were all reasons to celebrate. When a young girl became a woman, the entire clan celebrated. Each night the women danced and chanted around the girl's special hut. They imitated the movements of the **gemsbok**, a type of antelope, which they thought to be the most beautiful of all animals. On the celebration's final night, the men also danced. The young woman was then presented to the clan as an adult.

# SAN LANGUAGE

The San language has more sounds than most other languages, making it very hard for outsiders to learn. Experiment with making click sounds by putting your tongue on the roof of your mouth and clicking. Try moving your tongue to different places in your mouth and see how the click sounds change. See how many different click sounds you can make.

Around 1,500 years ago, Bantu groups arrived in southern Africa from central Africa. They brought livestock and crops. The Bantu were from different ethnic groups, but spoke similar languages like Swahili, Zulu, and Swazi. Many San were gradually absorbed into these groups and adopted their herding lifestyle.

The Dutch arrived in the 1600s, and began moving inland. Although the San had lived on these lands for thousands of years, the Europeans did not recognize their land rights. As the Dutch built roads, farms, and fences, the hunting and gathering San could no longer roam freely across the land for food. For many, the only choice was to work on the white farms. Others moved further inland to the Kalahari Desert.

**Over time, other African ethnic groups and then Europeans moved into San lands and affected the way the San lived.**

**WORDS TO KNOW**

**shuka:** red robe worn by Maasai warriors.

**Enkai:** god of the Maasai people.

Today, many San live in government settlements and work as wildlife park guides or on farms. Only a few clans in the Kalahari Desert still follow a traditional nomadic lifestyle. As the San have mingled and married into other groups, some of their customs have been lost. Their language and the stories passed down for thousands of years are not taught in schools. As San elders die, their knowledge of San history and culture dies with them.

# The Maasai

On the grasslands of Kenya or Tanzania, a young Maasai man guards his cattle. He stands tall and slim, with smooth brown skin. A red **shuka** hangs down his back and colorful beads circle his wrists, ankles, and neck. This picture could have been taken today or hundreds of years ago. Over the years, the Maasai lifestyle has changed very little.

**The name Maasai means "people who speak the Maa language."**

Historians believe the Maasai came from the Nile Valley to East Africa in the 1400s. They earned their reputation as fierce warriors, and driving out other ethnic groups. As herders, the Maasai brought their cattle to graze on the savanna.

**Ankole Cow**

Cattle are extremely important to Maasai society. A Maasai creation story says that **Enkai** sent cattle down to them from the sky along a bark rope. Another group that did not receive any cattle cut the rope, separating heaven and earth. This stopped the stream of cattle from Enkai. According to the story, all cattle belong to the Maasai. When Maasai warriors raided other groups and took their cattle, they did not see it as stealing. They were taking back what was theirs.

Cattle provide the Maasai with cow's milk and bull's blood. The Maasai carefully puncture the bull's neck with an arrow, collecting some of the bull's blood in a gourd. Because of their value and religious importance, cattle are rarely killed for food. They can be given as wedding gifts or traded for other goods.

Everyone in the family takes care of the cattle. The men and boys protect them from predators like lions. Women and young children milk and feed the cattle.

# MAASAI BEADED JEWELRY

Maasai people are famous for colorful beadwork. The women wear wide, flat, beaded collars that move rhythmically when they dance. Warriors decorate their wrists, ankles, necks, and waists with beaded bands. Traditionally, the Maasai women created jewelry out of local materials such as seeds, bone, gourds, and wood. After 1900, they used colorful glass and plastic beads from Europe. Each woman's piece illustrates her creativity. While most jewelry is created for beauty, some is used to mark special occasions. These include celebrations for engaged couples, successful lion hunts, or one of the many Maasai ceremonies.

Because cattle need fresh grass, the Maasai often travel for several weeks to reach new pastures. When they reach fertile land, they build a new village.

A Maasai village is called an **enkang.** Several families from the same clan live in an enkang. The married women build family huts from branches, twigs, and clay made from a mixture of cattle dung, urine, and mud. When the clay dries, it is as hard as cement and does not smell. Layers of dried grass on the roof keep the hut cool. The huts have one small doorway and a small opening in the roof or wall to allow smoke from a fire to escape. Ceilings are so low that adults cannot stand inside the hut. Beds made from woven branches are softened by grass and animal skins.

In Maasai culture, as in many other cultures around the world, one man may have several wives. Each wife has a hut for herself and her children. The enkang's huts form a circle around a large open area. The men protect the circle of huts by building a bush fence surrounding the entire village. Made from reeds and branches, the fence can be as sharp as barbed wire.

# MAASAI DANCING

Dancing is an important part of festivals and ceremonies. The adumu is a popular Maasai dance. A group of warriors stand in a circle, singing and chanting a rhythmic song. One at a time, the warriors move into the circle's center and jump up and down. The best dancers are the ones that jump the straightest and highest.

Several gates allow the village people to move in and out. At night, the men herd the clan's cattle through the fence into the center of the village. They close the gate to keep the clan and its cattle safe from wild animals.

A Maasai boy eats, plays, and works with boys in the same **age set**. As teenagers, boys and girls go through initiation ceremonies to celebrate becoming adults. After a group of boys from the same age set is initiated, they become junior warriors. They live in a **manyatta**.

Maasai warriors wear red cloaks and carry a spear and shield. With hair styled in long braids, the warriors decorate their bodies with colorful beaded jewelry and smear red paint on their faces and in their hair. Once the warriors stole cattle and led wars against neighboring groups. Today these practices are rare. Modern life in the manyatta is full of food, games, and practicing herding skills. Danger still exists from predators such as lions, though, so the warriors must acquire fighting skills.

For Maasai girls, the initiation ceremony means that she is ready to marry a village elder. Parents choose the elder. He pays the bride's family a bride price, usually in cattle. After the wedding, the young woman builds her home in her husband's village and focuses on family life and raising children.

The Maasai give their elders great respect. Once they reach the age of 30, warriors shave off their braids and become junior elders. The oldest and wisest men in the village are the senior elders.

**Maasai warriors wear the color red because it symbolizes their group and is believed to frighten lions.**

## WORDS TO KNOW

**enkang:** a Maasai village.

**age set:** a group of people born in the same year or group of years.

**manyatta:** a Maasai warrior village, separate from the main village or enkang.

Elders form a council that runs the village. Senior elders make decisions for the clan, settle disputes between clan members, and teach Maasai history and culture. The rest of the group takes care of the senior elders, cooking their meals and building and maintaining their homes.

The Maasai believe in one god, Enkai. The black Enkai is good and brings rains to re-plenish the grassy plains. The red Enkai is evil and brings lightning that can start wildfires and kill humans. When thunder rumbles, the Maasai believe the two sides of Enkai are fighting in the heavens. A wise man in the village is the clan's spiritual leader and healer.

Pressure from modern life is changing Maasai communities and their traditional lifestyles. Many no longer rely on cattle as their only source of income and food. Some have become farmers. Others hunt, fish, or earn money working in a city. Many wear modern pants and shirts and welcome modern amenities like electricity and running water in their villages.

**Older women also have a place of great respect. They have important roles in ceremonies and inform the senior elders of any problems in the community.**

Maasai women sell beaded jewelry and other crafts to tourists. Some villages have even opened their gates to allow groups of paying tourists to see village life first hand. As Kenya and Tanzania build new towns and roads, and set aside land in wildlife preserves, Maasai grazing lands shrink. They are no longer able to roam freely across the plains, and this is changing their traditions.

# MAKE YOUR OWN
## Rock Paintings

## SUPPLIES

- large rock
- pencil
- acrylic paints
- thin and thick paintbrushes

San artists are famous for their enduring rock and cave paintings. Now it's your turn to create a piece of art from your life and history.

**1** Think about what you'd like to paint. You could show a scene that tells the story of an important event in your life. Or paint about your dreams and goals in life. You could honor a parent, grandparent, aunt, or uncle. Whatever you decide, think about how to tell the story only in pictures. What objects should be large? Which should be smaller? What colors will you use? Remember, no words allowed!

**2** Paint your scene on the rock face. You might want to trace it first with a pencil. Use the different brushes and even your fingertips to create different types of paint lines and markings. Keep the figures simple—people in cave art were often drawn as stick figures.

**3** Once your painting has dried, see if your family and friends can read the message in your rock art painting.

## SAN CAVE PAINTINGS

Much of what we know about the San people comes from beautiful paintings on large rocks and cave walls. Thousands of paintings remain today in Namibia, Botswana, Lesotho, and South Africa. Scenes of hunting, gathering, animals, and dancing tell the history of the San. Some paintings show spirit creatures that are half human and half animal. Others show the arrival of the Bantu people and Europeans.

Only the best artists created the rock paintings. They traveled from clan to clan, receiving special treatment almost like Hollywood stars today. The artists used quills, feathers, sticks, bones, and fingers to paint. Some tools created thin lines while other tools made broader brush strokes. For paint, the artists crushed natural materials, like colored rock, into a powder. Iron oxide gave a red tint to the paint, white clay produced white paint, and charcoal made black paint. They mixed the powder with liquid such as egg whites, water, or blood to form the paint.

# MAKE YOUR OWN
## Maasai Beaded Necklace

The use of color in beaded designs is important to the Maasai. The designs are beautiful, and the colors symbolize elements of Maasai life, especially the importance of cattle. When choosing beads, a Maasai woman considers the following: Red means danger, ferocity, bravery, and strength. It also symbolizes unity, like the blood of a cow slaughtered for a community celebration. Blue is the color of the sky that gives water. White, the color of milk, is pure. Green is the color of the land that grows food for cattle to eat. Green also means health, like tall and plentiful plants. Orange and yellow represent hospitality, like the color of gourds of milk offered to visitors or the animal skins on a visitor's bed. Black is the color of the people and symbolizes the hardships of everyday life.

**1** Look at pictures of colorful Maasai jewelry. Decide what colors and patterns you want to use in your necklace. Remember that each color has a special meaning and significance. If you don't have a paper plate, you can use heavyweight paper or a piece of cardboard instead. Use a pencil to trace a dinner plate on the paper or cardboard and cut out the circle shape.

**2** Take the paper plate or circle and measure about 3 inches (7–8 centimeters) from the rim, making a mark with your pencil. Repeat several times around the plate. Connect your markings to draw an inner circle on the plate. Cut a straight line from the edge of the plate to the penciled circle. Cut the inner circle out following the pencil lines. This opening will become your necklace's neck hole. If the hole is too small for your neck, use your scissors to carefully cut a little more of the plate away, expanding the neck hole.

## SUPPLIES

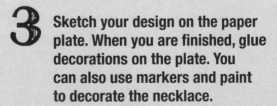

- pictures of Maasai jewelry from the Internet or a book or magazine
- plain white paper plates, cardboard, and heavyweight paper
- pencil
- scissors
- ruler
- glue
- decorating items including colorful beads, small stones, hard pasta shapes, seeds
- markers or paints

**3** Sketch your design on the paper plate. When you are finished, glue decorations on the plate. You can also use markers and paint to decorate the necklace.

**4** Make additional necklaces to stack around your neck like the Maasai. Vary the size of the necklace each time.

### Chapter 7

# HOMES

**L**ike many things in Africa, the type of home you live in depends on where you live. In large cities like Nairobi, Kenya, and Johannesburg, South Africa, people live in towering apartment buildings, townhouses, and single-family homes. They're not that much different from many American homes. Houses in older neighborhoods are often crowded together, with no yards. In wealthier areas, colonial mansions built by Europeans are two stories tall and have large, wrap-around verandas or porches.

In rural areas and villages, African homes are usually built with local materials such as mud, wood, grass, animal skins, and hides. There are no professional house builders in a village. Most men and women in the village can build a house themselves. If someone is too old and sick to build a house, then the village people will pitch in and build one for them.

Traditional African houses are round, with a cone-shaped roof. Some villages will also create square or rectangular houses with a steep roof that rain runs off easily.

Although each ethnic group adds its own special features, the basic design is similar. The house is one simple room, with no electricity or running water. When a new room is needed, the family builds another house. Several houses are often grouped together around an open **courtyard**. The family compound's courtyard is a busy place for cooking, playing, and chores.

In a typical compound, one house is the sleeping area for the head of the family. Older sons have their own sleeping houses. Children and unmarried girls sleep with their mothers. Storage huts for grains and vegetables are a sign of wealth. If the family has livestock, sections of the compound serve as pens for the animals. Walls separate compounds in a village.

To build a house, the men gather supplies in the bush and forest. They search for short, strong, wooden branches for walls and longer, thinner, flexible branches for horizontal beams. Long wood poles create roof rafters. The men gather long grasses to **thatch** the roof.

## WORDS TO KNOW

**courtyard:** an open space surrounded by walls or buildings.

**thatch:** to cover a roof with a material such as long grasses, straw, or leaves.

**insulate:** keep hot or cool air inside.

**shantytown:** settlements of shacks.

**erosion:** slowly wear away.

Wood poles covered with a mixture of grass and mud, called wattle and daub, is a common building method, used for over 6,000 years.

Back in the village, the men set slender tree trunks in the ground in the shape they want the house to be. They tie the thinner, more flexible branches in a horizontal framework around the house. A packed mud mixture along the framework creates solid walls. In the hot sun, the mud dries and hardens. Because mud pulls away from openings as it dries, the homes often have only a single door.

To construct a roof, the men use long wooden poles tied in several places with wire or tree bark string. Thatching the roof using long grass or reeds tied in bundles helps **insulate** and cool the home.

Once the structure is complete, the walls are plastered inside and out with a mud or clay mixture. The builder soaks the dirt floor, then packs, beats, and smooths it. This produces a firm, hard, even floor. Today, some people use a cement plaster on the floor.

A typical home can be finished in a few days. The family might spread woven mats and animal skins on the floor. They may hang blankets or skins from the roof rafters to divide the room into sections for privacy. Some societies hang offerings or charms made from animal horns, shells, and feathers to ward off evil spirits.

Using mud to build houses in Africa has many advantages. Mud homes cost little to build and maintain.

**The rope used to tie the wooden framework together is often made from tree bark. The builder soaks it in water, then ties the wood beams and rafters together while it is still wet. As the bark dries it shrinks, tightly pulling the beams together.**

# SHANTYTOWNS

One disadvantage to modern life in Africa has been the growth of **shantytowns** on the outskirts of cities. Many poor workers cannot afford housing so they build shelters using whatever materials they can find. Homes in shantytowns are made of scrap wood, metal, and plastic. Shantytowns are known for danger, poverty, crime, and disease. These communities are built illegally, and have no police, fire fighters, or medical services. Buildings are flammable and built close together, so dangerous fires can spread quickly. With no running water, shantytown residents must buy their daily water. Vendors take advantage of residents by selling water at inflated prices. Sitting in the shadows of cities, shantytowns show the divide between Africa's haves and have nots.

They are well suited to the hot, dry African climate. When built on a strong foundation, mud is a sturdy material. It can withstand heavy rains as long as the sun dries it afterwards. Mud is also easy to work with and decorate.

In areas where other building materials are expensive and scarce, mud is inexpensive, eco-friendly, and plentiful. Where wood is scarce, like Northern Africa, the walls may be made entirely of mud bricks.

Today's builders may use modern tools like saws and axes. Some villages construct metal roofs or use stone and brick in their houses. Others add concrete to mud mixtures for added strength. But the basic form of the traditional African house remains the same.

Living in a mud house does have some disadvantages. The houses are small. The single door opening makes it dark and stuffy inside. Some builders prop up the roof, leaving a gap between the top of the walls and the roof. This allows more air and light to circulate through the house.

**Erosion** also wears away mud walls over time. Therefore, mud houses need maintenance and re-plastering to protect the structure.

Some people think mud houses are primitive and backward. To these people, houses made of concrete, steel, and glass are symbols of progress, while mud represents the past. Because of the benefits to using mud, efforts are being made throughout Africa to overcome the negative perception of mud houses.

# MAKE YOUR OWN
## Ndebele House Painting

The Ndebele people of southern Africa are famous for colorful, geometric designs painted on their houses. Traditionally they used homemade paint to decorate walls, doorframes, and window frames. They also dragged their fingers through wet cow dung plaster to create lines, squiggles, and zigzag patterns. The Ndebele believed this type of painting created a connection between the past, present, and future. Some believed bad luck and sickness would befall those who did not honor their ancestors in this way. Today the Ndebele incorporate details from their everyday lives along with traditional patterns. Often, a woman's house painting will include images of items they want to own someday. A wall painting can tell can the story of the painter's aspirations and desires.

## SUPPLIES

- pictures of Ndebele houses from the Internet
- large piece of white paper or poster board—you can tape several pieces together to create a large canvas
- pencil
- ruler or yardstick
- thick black marker
- paint and brushes or markers

**1** Study pictures of traditional Ndebele geometric designs to help you find ideas for how you want to decorate your canvas.

**2** Using a pencil, sketch out your house design on the white paper. Use the ruler to create straight lines and geometric shapes. Try to make your design and shapes symmetrical—the same on the right and left.

**3** Once the design is complete, use a thick black marker to trace over your pencil lines. Then use paint or markers to color in sections of the design. Remember that some sections should be left white to contrast with the colored sections. Decorate your wall with your house painting.

# MAKE YOUR OWN
## African Family Compound

**1** Sketch the outline of the compound on the cardboard. How many buildings will your compound have? There are usually several sleeping huts, and storage huts for grains and vegetables. Show where each hut will stand. Make pen areas for livestock, and trace the outline of the wall that separates the family compound from other compounds.

**2** Use the clay to create traditional round huts. Form the roofs into cone shapes. Use clay to shape the compound's wall.

**3** Once the compound's structure is complete, add animal and people figures. Some family members may be cooking in the compound's center area, while others herd livestock into their pens.

## SUPPLIES

- large piece of cardboard
- pencil
- modeling clay

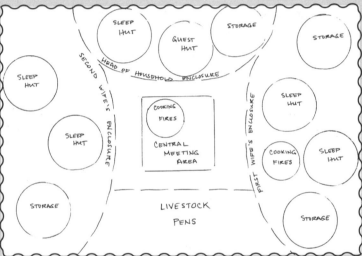

## OTHER TYPES OF HOMES

Throughout Africa, people adapt their homes to fit their lifestyle and the available resources. In low-lying river areas prone to flooding, people live in houses set high on stilts over the water. In some regions, houses may use stone as a building material.

While permanent mud homes work well for a farming community, they don't make sense for hunters and gatherers that are always on the move. In the Sahara desert, people leading a nomadic life bend flexible branches into domes and cover them with fabric and leather to protect against the scorching sun and cold nights. They take the shelter with them as they move. At the next stop, they assemble the shelter again.

### Chapter 8

# FOOD & DAILY LIFE

**L**ife in Africa can be as different as a slithering snake and a thundering elephant. It varies from region to region, from modern cities to rural villages. Teens in Africa's largest cities, like Nairobi, might live in three-bedroom houses and attend private schools. They listen to iPods, ride mountain bikes, surf the Internet, and play video games.

## Chores and school

The majority of Africans, however, live in smaller, more rural villages. For these people, daily life follows a more traditional pattern. For example, when day dawns in one African village, a young girl might leave her family's compound carrying two large containers. Because her house doesn't have running water, she must collect water each day. In some villages, the community water pump or well is just down the street.

The difference in lifestyle between African teens can be enormous. One girl, living a nomadic lifestyle, spends her evening by the fire listening to traditional stories handed down from her ancestors. Another girl, living in a South African city, reads her favorite Harry Potter book under electric lights.

In others, it might be several miles to a river or spring. If cattle drink from the water source they will contaminate it. Families will then have to boil their water before using it or risk getting sick.

A toilet is often a hole dug in the ground outside a home. Without showers or bathtubs, children wash by splashing their bodies with water from a small bowl.

After doing their chores, children might walk several miles to attend school. Many village schools are one big room, where all the students learn together. Other schools gather on benches under a shady tree.

## Children in Tanzania can spend 2 hours a day collecting water.

Unfortunately, many village children in Africa only go to school for a few years or don't go at all. Many families cannot afford the school fees. Families might send their boys to school but keep the girls at home to work. Today, nonprofit groups help many families pay for school fees. Other groups raise money to build schools in villages to make education available to more children.

After school, children help their mothers. As more village men travel to cities to work and earn money, the women left behind take on more work in the village. They are the backbone of the community. The women work in the fields and go to market. They perform all the day-to-day household chores.

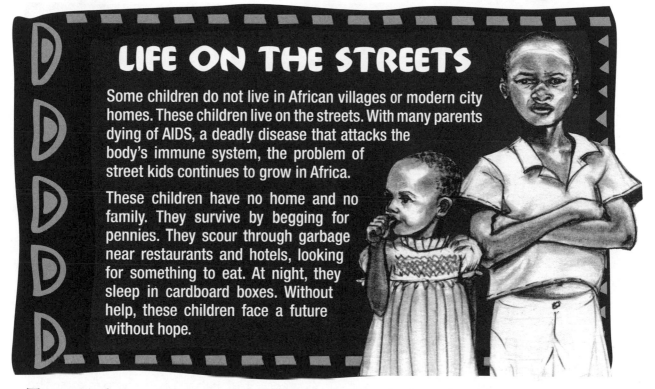

## LIFE ON THE STREETS

Some children do not live in African villages or modern city homes. These children live on the streets. With many parents dying of AIDS, a deadly disease that attacks the body's immune system, the problem of street kids continues to grow in Africa.

These children have no home and no family. They survive by begging for pennies. They scour through garbage near restaurants and hotels, looking for something to eat. At night, they sleep in cardboard boxes. Without help, these children face a future without hope.

This includes sweeping and washing, preparing food, and taking care of the children. Some village women also make crafts to sell to tourists. Others work in shops, markets, or as teachers. Despite the important work African women do, many societies still do not treat men and women equally.

In Ethiopia, you can eat the tablecloth! The tables are covered with overlapping pieces of injera, a flatbread. Diners break off pieces of injera and wrap it around meat or stew.

# Food

In the country, most people live almost entirely on food they grow or find themselves. There are no fast food restaurants. No supermarkets. Instead, villagers grow grains, vegetables, and fruit in fields and gardens. They catch fish in rivers and lakes. Village men snare and hunt game for meat. The food in each village varies depending on the land's natural resources.

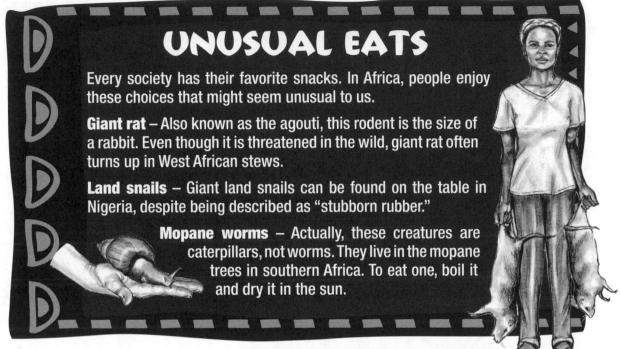

## UNUSUAL EATS

Every society has their favorite snacks. In Africa, people enjoy these choices that might seem unusual to us.

**Giant rat** – Also known as the agouti, this rodent is the size of a rabbit. Even though it is threatened in the wild, giant rat often turns up in West African stews.

**Land snails** – Giant land snails can be found on the table in Nigeria, despite being described as "stubborn rubber."

**Mopane worms** – Actually, these creatures are caterpillars, not worms. They live in the mopane trees in southern Africa. To eat one, boil it and dry it in the sun.

Just about everyone helps out in the fields. The entire family helps plow, clear land, collect firewood, weed, and carry produce back to the compound. If the family has sheep, goats, and maybe a cow for milk, the children help lead the animals to grazing lands.

In an African city, a family living in an apartment may have a kitchen like one you'd see in the United States. In rural villages the kitchen is usually outside or in a separate building in the family's compound. A large black pot set on three stones arranged in a triangle is the most common way to cook. Pieces of wood meet at a point under the pot and slowly feed the cooking fire.

Women stir the pot with wooden stirrers and teach their daughters how to prepare the family meals. Girls learn a variety of cooking methods like steaming in leaves, or grilling and roasting meat.

Yams are one of the oldest foods grown in Africa. Because new yams grow from old sprouted yams, the yam is a symbol of renewal and rebirth. Many regions hold annual yam festivals to celebrate.

## WORDS TO KNOW

**fufu:** a thick porridge or paste made with yams, cassava, or grains.

**mortar:** a bowl used for grinding or crushing grain.

**pestle:** a long stick or pole used to pound or grind grain in a mortar bowl.

Across Africa, **fufu** is a staple food in many homes. Fufu is a thick porridge or paste similar to mashed potatoes. In Western and Central Africa, the women make fufu from yams or cassava. They boil the starchy root vegetables, then pound them with a stick until the fufu is thick and smooth.

In other areas of Africa, women make fufu using ground corn flour or other grains instead of root vegetables. They grind the grain using a large wooden **mortar** and stone **pestle**. Grinding the grain takes a lot of time and energy. Some women rise before dawn to grind grain. Adding boiled water and vigorous stirring makes a porridge-like meal that is thick and smooth. Each region has different names for fufu. It is called ugali in Kenya and Tanzania, mshma in Zambia, and sadza in Zimbabwe.

A thick or soupy stew is frequently the centerpiece of an African meal. The women prepare the stew with vegetables such as okra, yams, cassava, beans, peas, and onions. Meat or fish is added if it is available. Sometimes spices and chilies flavor the stew.

## BANANAS IN AFRICA

Bananas came to Africa about 2,000 years ago from Southeast Asia. Today, bananas are found in almost all areas of Africa south of the Sahara. Bananas are popular because they are easy to grow and require little labor. A well-maintained banana garden can yield fruit for 30 or more years. Bananas are very nutritious—you could live indefinitely eating only milk and bananas. A cousin of the banana, the plantain, is also found in Africa. Plantains are often roasted or mashed. In Tanzania and Uganda, plantains are fermented into beer.

Eating in Africa is a communal event. Often everyone sits together outside to share the meal. The women and girls serve the meal in wooden bowls. Made by the family, these bowls may be simple or highly decorated.

**While eating sweets in growing more common in Africa, dessert is not part of the traditional African meal. Instead, a piece of mango or pineapple might be eaten at the end of a meal.**

Africans often use their hands when eating fufu. The diner tears off a small piece of the sticky fufu and rolls it into a ball. He uses his thumb to make an indentation in the ball, and then dips it into a stew or sauce. The indentation holds a bit of the stew's liquid to enjoy with the fufu. In some countries, like Nigeria, the diner swallows the ball whole.

In Senegal, the typical meal is served on a long tray. The family sits around the tray and helps themselves. There are no utensils, so each family member makes sure to wash their hands in a little bowl of water before and after the meal. Because it is considered rude in Senegal to reach, family members break off pieces of meat, fish, and vegetables and toss them in front of each person.

# BASKET MAKING

If you need something in an African village, you make it yourself. Baskets are a common household item that African women create for a variety of uses. Large baskets store extra food and grains. Smaller baskets can hold milk for children to drink.

Weaving is a timeless method of creating baskets. The women gather long strands of grass to weave over and under each other, forming the bottom and sides of the basket. By alternating grass dyed in different colors, the designer can weave stripes and other designs into the basket.

# THE ART OF POTTERY

Not all African pots are used for cooking or storage. Some are for religious or marriage ceremonies. A potter might sculpt a human head or figure to rest on top of the pot. Or decorate other pots with a complex pattern. In southern Ghana, the Asante people traditionally made special pots called family pots for funerals. They decorated black pots with symbols and images of animals, birds, and human heads to help in the transition to the afterlife. During the funeral ceremony, the family shaved their heads and put their hair into the pot. They carried the pot to a special burial ground and recited a final blessing.

## Storage Containers

African women use a variety of containers to store food. Dried and hollowed **calabash** gourds make good containers for grains and vegetables. Clay pots keep water cool. In some regions, the women pierce the ends of large, empty ostrich eggshells to use as water or milk carriers. Containers are set on shelves or hung from ropes to protect the food from mice, rats, and snakes.

### WORDS TO KNOW

**calabash:** a bottle-shaped gourd.

**coiling:** winding in a ring shape.

**burnish:** polish with friction to make smooth and bright.

**haggle:** bargain for a lower price.

Clay pots are used for cooking, holding water, and storage. Making pots is usually a woman's job. A popular way to make pots is by **coiling**. First the potter forms clay into a large, sausage-like roll and joins the two ends into a circle or coil. Small pots may use only one coil, while larger ones may use two or three. The potter shapes the pot by squeezing and pulling sections of the clay upwards.

When the pot is formed, the potter may beat it with a wooden spatula to create a smoother shape. **Burnishing** the outside of the pot with a smooth stone seals it and makes it better able to hold water. While the clay is still damp, the potter may add decorations such as lines, dots, or symbols to her design.

After the pot dries in the hot sun, the potter fires it in a bonfire, with several other pots. Once the fire burns out and the pots cool, they are ready to use.

# Markets

In a rural village, the women go to a local market almost every day to get supplies. African markets are colorful, noisy places with booths selling food, crafts, livestock, and cloth. Buyers and sellers trade and **haggle** over prices until they each get what they want. If the rains have been good and there are extra crops, a family may sell or trade their produce at the market. Otherwise, they use the crops to feed themselves only.

# Getting Together

Without electricity, families don't relax in front of the television after dinner. In fact, there are no televisions, video games, or computers in many village homes. At night, wax candles and kerosene lanterns might provide the only light. Visiting friends, telling stories, and singing and making music are all popular things to do after the sun goes down.

In rural villages, extended families play an important role. Aunts, uncles, cousins, and grandparents often live nearby, either in the same village, or within a day's walk. Most Africans think nothing of a six-hour walk to visit family. African village children feel the love of an entire extended family, learning from each member and helping each other out during times of trouble.

In some West African villages, the men relax and talk about village issues in an open-air structure with shaded seats called a bantaba.

# MAKE YOUR OWN
## Zitumbuwa (Banana Fritters)

## SUPPLIES

- ripe bananas
- spoon and bowl for mashing
- pinch ot salt
- 1 teaspoon sugar
- ½ cup cornmeal (also known as ufa)
- cooking oil
- fry pan
- slotted spoon
- paper towels
- butter or sugar (optional)

You'll be using the stove for this activity, so ask a grown-up for help!

**1** Mash the bananas well. Mix in the salt, sugar and cornmeal. Heal oil in a deep fry pan. Add spoonfuls of the banana mixture to the hot oil. Be very careful not to burn yourself! When the bottom turns a light golden color, flip the fritter to cook the other side.

**2** Remove the fritters with a slotted spoon and place on paper towels to absorb any excess oil. Enjoy your fritters warm with butter or rolled in sugar. Dig in!

# MAKE YOUR OWN
## African FuFu

You'll need to use the stove to boil the yams and a knife for cutting, so ask a grown-up for help.

**1** Peel and cut the yams into several pieces. Boil the yam pieces until they are soft.

**2** Put the boiled yams in a large, heavy mixing bowl one at a time. Mash them with a potato masher. Gradually add the other pieces of yams and keep mashing. Add a few spoonfuls of hot water to the mixture from time to time to keep it moist. Don't use too much water, the fufu should be thick.

## SUPPLIES

- several yams
- vegetable peeler & knife
- pot of boiling water
- heavy mixing bowl
- potato masher
- a few spoonfuls of hot water

**3** When you've finished pounding the yams, roll the fufu into about a dozen 2-inch balls. Serve your fufu balls in a bowl with a dipping sauce, soup, or stew.

# MAKE YOUR OWN
## Basket

**1** Cut eight strips of construction paper from your first color. Each strip should be 12 inches (30.5 centimeters) long and ¾ inch (2 centimeters) wide.

**2** Glue the edges of two pieces of a second color of construction paper together. When the glue has dried, cut four strips measuring 16 inches (41 centimeters) long and ½ inch (1 centimeter) wide.

**3** Glue 2 strips from your first color in the shape of a cross. Repeat this with your remaining first color strips, until you have four crosses. Lay the four crosses on top of each other, with the strips fanning out like a star. Glue in place.

**4** Lay the plate face down on a piece of construction paper. Trace the plate's outline with a pencil. Cut out the plate shape and glue on top of your strip star.

**5** Bend the edges or rays of the star strips up around the circle's edge. Tape a strip from your second color across the bottom of one ray. Weave that strip over and under the star's ray strips. When you reach where you started, tape the other end of the woven strip to a ray.

## SUPPLIES

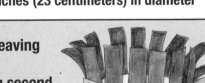

- several sheets of construction paper in at least two colors
- ruler
- scissors
- glue stick
- plate, 5 inches (12 to 13 centimeters) in diameter
- pencil
- tape
- large plate, 9 inches (23 centimeters) in diameter

**6** Repeat weaving with your remaining second color strips. Alternate the over and under on each ray. Make sure to keep the strips close together. When you've finished weaving all four strips, fold any remaining pieces of the ray strips down and secure with tape or glue inside the basket. This forms your basket's rim.

**7** To make a lid for your basket, trace a larger plate on construction paper. Cut a wedge like a piece of pie out of the circle. Now pull the two ends of your circle together and glue or tape. This should form a cone-like structure that can be used as a basket lid.

**Variation:** Decorate your basket with paint or markers.

### Chapter 9

# GAMES & TOYS

**L**ike children all around the world, African children play with toys and games. However, it is hard to find a toy store in an African village. Instead of buying the latest trendy toy, African children use imagination and creativity to make their own toys and games.

Children use everyday objects around them to make toys. Those who live in sandy areas may dig holes for a game board. Game pieces can be made from rocks and shells. A pile of rags tied together with twine may become a soccer ball. Just about any object is fair game for the children to use.

One type of homemade toy is a **galimoto**. Children build these push toys from old wires, sticks, cornstalks, pieces of yarn, or whatever materials the children can find. They shape these items into cars, trucks, bicycles, trains, and helicopters.

**The word galimoto means car in Chichewa, the national language of Malawi.**

Galimotos may also have a stick or string attached that allows children to push or pull them along the ground.

Boys in Africa like to drum, roll hoops (or rims or tires), and play sports like soccer and baseball. In many areas, the young men also like to wrestle. Sometimes crowds of people from the community will gather to watch the wrestling matches. Traditionally, some African boys also play war games. These games teach the boys the strength and skills needed to become warriors. Some ethnic groups, like the Zulu, use long sticks in a fencing-like game to show the boys how to strike and avoid blows.

 **In the Ndebele ethnic group of southern Africa, a young man will place a doll outside the hut of a young woman to propose marriage.**

African girls enjoy jumping rope, hopscotch, and playing a form of jacks using small stones. Many girls also have handmade dolls. The doll's maker may use wood, beads, wax, nails, and fabric to decorate the doll.

Both boys and girls enjoy playing marbles using seeds, nuts, stones, or dried fruit. There is also a lot of singing, dancing, and playing music. Because much of Africa is hot and dry, children play outside. They spend a lot of time in large groups so fewer adults are needed to watch them. This leads to many physical games for large numbers of kids.

Most games, especially in the rural areas of Africa, don't require equipment. If they do need something for their game, the children might use a tool from nature like stones, sticks, leaves, and feathers.

## WORDS TO KNOW

**galimoto:** a homemade push toy.

**ritual:** a set of actions performed the same way each time.

**fertility:** being able to have children.

## DOLLS

While many dolls are simply for fun, others have a special purpose in **rituals** and religion. Some dolls are used in initiation ceremonies that welcome a girl into womanhood. In many African societies, dolls symbolize **fertility**. These fertility dolls are a type of good luck charm, helping the girl to grow up to become a mother with healthy babies. Fertility dolls are often handed down from mother to daughter.

One popular game is called Kameshi Ne Mpuku, or the Cat and the Rat. Children play variations of this game throughout Africa. Players from the Congo's Luba people line up in four equal rows, holding hands in each row. Three children are chosen to be the caller, the rat, and the cat.

When the game begins, the rat runs up and down the aisles between the rows and the cat chases. When the caller shouts "Mpuki ekale" or "let the rat stop," the children in the rows release hands and grab hands with the row across from them. This forms the rows in a new direction. The rat must react quickly to the change or find himself trapped in the hands. As the game continues, the caller keeps changing the direction of the rows. When the rat is caught or time is up, the game is over.

Many traditional African games teach the children skills that are valued by their community. The games reward good judgment, quickness, decision-making, and agility.

Another popular activity for African children is playing string games. The string figures represent people, places, animals, and important objects. Children wrap string around their fingers in complex patterns to form a shape. Usually, the children choose to make shapes of objects found near their homes like a bird's nest, snakes climbing a tree, or diamonds. During storytelling, string figures illustrate stories.

# MAKE YOUR OWN
## Mancala Game

Africans, young and old, enjoy board games. Hundreds of ethnic groups across Africa play Mancala, one of the oldest board games in the world. It is a mathematical game that uses strategy and counting. Each ethnic group has a special name for the game and plays it with a slightly different variation.

The Mancala game board is usually wooden with rows of cups or holes that hold seeds, pebbles, or other small pieces. A game board may have two, three, or four rows of holes. If a traditional wooden board is not available, people can play the game using seashells and holes in the ground. You can make your own Mancala game using everyday items from your kitchen.

## SUPPLIES

- empty egg cartons
- scissors
- tape
- paint or markers
- 36 dried beans, nuts, pebbles, or beads to use as game pieces

**1** Cut the lid off one egg carton so that you just have the side with the egg holes.

**2** Cut two egg cups from a second egg carton. Use tape to attach one cup to each end of your first egg carton. These will be your end cups, called your mancala. As you win game pieces, you'll store them in your mancala.

**3** Decorate your Mancala board with paint or markers. You can draw patterns, symbols, letters, and numbers.

**4** To set up the game, place the board between two players. Each player "owns" the six cups on the side nearest to them and the end cup to their right. During the game, you can move the pieces from your side of the board, but not the pieces on your opponent's side. Place three game pieces in each of the 12 game cups. Leave the end cups empty. Now you're ready to play!

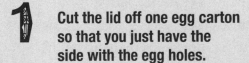

The Mancala game is called Bao in East Africa, Oware in Ghana, and Ayo in Nigeria.

The object of Mancala is to move your pieces from hole to hole around the board, gathering more pieces than your opponent. Follow the rules below and challenge your family to a game!

**1** Choose a player to go first. You might pick the youngest or the one whose birthday is closest. That player scoops up all the game pieces from one cup on their side of the board. Moving to the right, the player drops one piece in each cup along the board. If the player comes to their own end cup, they should drop a piece in there. If the player still has pieces in their hand, they continue moving along the board and drops those pieces one at a time into their opponent's cups. If the player reaches their opponent's end cup, they should skip over it. If the player's last piccc falls in their own end cup, they get another turn. If not, it is the other player's turn.

**2** The second player chooses a cup on his side to empty and repeats what the first player did. The two players alternate turns. If a player drops his last piece into an empty cup on his own side, he can "capture" his opponent's pieces in the cup opposite the empty one. Players place captured pieces in their end cups. Then it is the other player's turn.

**3** The game is over when one player empties all six cups on his side. If the other player's cups still have pieces in them, that player places them into his own end cup. Then both players count the pieces in their end cups. The one with the most is the winner!

**Variation:** After you've played the game, try making up your own rules. You can change the number of game pieces or change the rules for capturing pieces. African communities have developed their own ways to play Mancala. Experiment and decide what version of the game you like best!

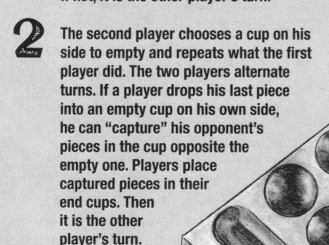

# MAKE YOUR OWN
## Soccer Ball

African children love to play soccer, which they call football. Many don't have store-bought balls. Instead, the children use materials they have at home, like rags and twine, to make their own soccer ball.

## SUPPLIES

- several rags or old T-shirts
- twine or string
- scissors

**1** Scrunch up several rags tightly into a ball. Wrap another rag around the surface of the scrunched ball of rags. Make sure you keep holding the ball tightly. Wrap as many wrags around as you like.

**2** When your ball is the size you want it, take the twine or string and wrap it around the ball several times. Use the twine to keep the rags together and in a ball shape by wrapping the twine around and around in several directions. The tighter you wrap the ball, the stronger and longer-lasting it will be. Try to make sure no rag pieces are hanging out and the strings are tight. When you are done wrapping the ball in twine, secure or tie the end pieces together.

Now it is time to test your ball. Take it outside and kick it around!

## 2010 WORLD CUP

In 2010, soccer's greatest tournament, the World Cup, comes to South Africa. It is the first time this international event has taken place on the African continent. The championship soccer tournament has been held every four years since 1930, except during World War II.

The qualification phase takes place during the three years before the actual tournament. Tournaments held around the world narrow the field of competing teams from 200 down to 32 teams. These 32 teams compete in the World Cup. The host nation, South Africa in 2010, is guaranteed a spot in the final stages of the competition. Do you think the 94 million people watching the Super Bowl is a big deal? Not even close! More than 715 million people around the globe watched the World Cup in 2006.

### Chapter 10

# CLOTHING & ADORNMENT

**T**he way a person dresses in Africa says a lot about who they are. Clothes provide more than protection against the sun, cold, and rain. They give clues about the wearer's position in society, ethnic group, age, occupation, and marital status. Do they live in a city or a village? Are they Maasai or Yoruba? Married or single? Are they an elder in their village? Looking at their clothes, you might be able to figure it out.

Many African societies believe appearance is important. **Adornments** and clothing are often bold and colorful. They express an individual's creativity. Cloth, leather, shells, beads, metals, and plant fibers make the body a living piece of art. Each piece sends a message depending on the material, pattern, color, and embroidery.

In modern times, many Africans wear Western-style clothing. Some, however, still dress in traditional ways. Others create their own style, blending Western and traditional African styles.

Clothing in Africa can vary from region to region. Some African men wear tailored cotton **tunics** and robes over a pair of loose-fitting pants. For Hausa men in Nigeria, a large, elaborately embroidered gown shows their important status. Woven caps that match the outfit are popular in these regions.

In other areas, men wear more unstructured clothing. In parts of Ghana and Ivory Coast, men's clothing consists of a large, rectangular piece of cloth. The man wraps the cloth around his body and drapes it over his left shoulder like a toga.

**Expensive kente cloth sends a message that the wearer may be wealthy or have a high position in society.**

Many African women wear a large rectangular piece of cloth wrapped around the body as a dress. At home, the woman may wear a single wrapper, but may add additional layers when she goes out in public. Some wear cotton wrappers with blouses made of matching fabrics. In Western Africa, many women also wrap their heads in matching fabric. The bigger and more elaborate the headdress, the more important the woman.

Traditional shoes in Africa are made from a variety of materials. Wood sandals and clogs protect feet from the hot sand and ground plants.

**WORDS TO KNOW**

**adornment:** jewelry or other decorations to make the body beautiful.

**tunic:** a gown-like outer garment, with or without sleeves.

**kente cloth:** fabric from Ghana made from colorful interwoven strips of cloth.

# KENTE CLOTH

Kente cloth is traditionally made by the Asante and other West African ethnic groups in Ghana. This world-famous cloth is made by weaving narrow strips on a loom. It's a time-consuming process. A weaver may work on a single garment for months. Because of this process, kente cloth is very expensive.

Kente cloth features blocks of patterns and bright colors. Each pattern has a name and meaning. The names come from African proverbs, sayings, historical events, and social customs. When a cloth has many different designs and colors it may be called adwinasa, which means all the motifs have been used up.

Historically, only rich and powerful kings and chiefs wore kente cloth at special social and religious ceremonies. Today, men and women all across society might wear clothing made of kente cloth. It is still a status symbol and worn during community celebrations and festivals.

Kente Cloth

Leather shoes can be worn in many different types of weather. Some northern people wear boots made with a leather sole and an upper section of colorful woven wool.

In many African societies, a woman's clothing tells whether she is married or not. An unmarried Kraramojong girl in Uganda wears a hip skirt and head ornaments. Once she marries, she joins other married women wearing a leather cloak and a skirt that ties in front.

Many African societies see a person's head as their spiritual center. Hair is an important symbol. African hair traditions mark a child's initiation into adulthood or show social status. To protect against evil spirits, the Sande people braid hollowed horns from antelope, goats, and sheep into their hair. Medicine herbs in the horns drive away the spirits.

Wooden combs are often carved with ornate designs and may be worn as a hair ornament.

The status of Maasai warriors is demonstrated by their long braids. The warriors carefully braid their hair into dreadlocks and smear it with red ocher and oil. When they become elders, shaving off their hair signals their new status.

The Yoruba people of Nigeria shave a newborn baby's head to separate the child from the spiritual world. When a Yoruba dies, their head is shaved again to mark their return to the spiritual world. Other groups, like the Maasai, shave the heads of young men and women as part of initiation ceremonies. Shaving is a symbol of rebirth, of stepping into adulthood.

Africans are known for wearing jewelry and accessories. In many regions, the more pieces a person wears, the more prestige and wealth they have. Jewelry might be made of valuable materials like ivory, bronze, or gold.

# BEADWORK

Africans are famous for their colorful beadwork. Different necklaces, earrings, aprons, and headdresses symbolize the wearer's status, ethnic group, and age. Maasai women wear flat, beaded collars to show they are ready for marriage. Married Maasai woman can wear a Nborro, a string of long blue beads. Maasai warriors wear beaded armbands and leg bands made by their mothers and girlfriends. When the warrior becomes an elder, he must remove his beaded jewelry.

The types of beads and patterns used can carry special meanings that vary from region to region. In some areas, cowrie beads represent fertility. In South Africa's Zulu beadwork, a triangle's three points represent the father, mother, and child. A triangle pointed down means the wearer is unmarried. Married women wear beadwork with two joined triangles in the shape of a diamond. Two triangles that form an X symbolize a married man.

Asante rulers wore many gold necklaces, anklets, arm bands, and rings. The oba of Benin wore coral jewelry and decorations to symbolize his royal status.

Some African groups decorate their bodies. Because the Surma people of Ethiopia wear little clothing, they express their creativity with their bodies as an art canvas. Men, women, and children smear chalk from the riverbed on their bodies. Drawing intricate designs with their fingertips reveals the dark skin underneath.

**In Northern and Western Africa, some people paint intricate designs on their hands, face, and feet with henna dye.**

The practice of **scarification** is an ancient body art in Africa. Cutting their skin with knives creates raised marks and patterns. Rubbing ashes into the cuts makes the scars heavier and more distinct. Some believe body scars are a symbol of beauty and a test of courage. In modern Africa, the practice of scarring has become less common.

**Beaded aprons in Cameroon show the changes in a woman's life—initiation, marriage, and widowhood.**

Some societies value specific body parts. Kikuyu and Maasai women of Kenya pierce and stretch their earlobes as a symbol of beauty. Young Ethiopian women of the Surma and Mursi pierce and stretch their lips. At age 15, girls place a wooden plug into a freshly pierced hole. Gradually, they increase the size of the plug, stretching out their lip. Eventually, the stretched lip holds a lip plate or disk. Wearing a large lip plate is a sign of beauty in their society. The Mursi women decorate their lip plates to create an intricate piece of art.

**WORDS TO KNOW**

**scarification:** the act of scarring or scratching the body.

# MAKE YOUR OWN
## Kente Strip Weaving

## SUPPLIES

- cardboard, about 8 x 10 inches (20 x 25 centimeters)
- scissors
- yarn in several colors
- long yarn needle
- wide-toothed comb

**1** To make your loom, cut notches in the cardboard close together along the two short sides. The notches should be no more than two-tenths of an inch apart (5 millimeters).

**2** Cut a piece of yarn approximately 3 feet (1 meter) long. Knot one end of the yarn and pull it through one of the end slits in your cardboard loom. The knot should anchor the yarn to the loom.

**3** Loop the yarn tightly down to the first notch on the bottom of the card. Wind it around the back of the card and back up to the second notch at the top. Continue winding your yarn through all the notches on your card. Keep your yarn tight. When you wind through the last notch, knot the yarn to anchor this end to the loom.

**4** Now that your loom is ready, it's time to weave! Cut about 2 feet (½ meter) from one color of yarn and thread it into your needle. Weave your needle under the first string on your loom, then over the next. Continue across the loom in this under and over pattern. Once you've reached the end, turn your needle back in the opposite direction, and weave back across the loom. If you wove under the last string, weave the yarn over it this time as you weave back to the other side of the loom.

**5** Continue weaving across the loom. Make sure you don't pull the thread too tight or your kente strip will curl inwards. As you weave, use the comb to push the new row against completed rows.

**6** To change colors or add more yarn, tie a knot joining the two strands of yarn. Continue weaving and alternating colors until you've reached the length you want. When you've finished weaving, tie the end of your last piece of yarn to an end loom string.

**7** Cut the loom strings on the back of your loom. Knot pairs of loom strings close together to prevent your weaving from slipping apart. The knotted loom strings will form a fringe at both ends of your kente strip. Trim the fringe to whatever length you want.

# MAKE YOUR OWN
## Beaded Bracelet

You can use whatever colors you want or make multiple bracelets in different colors. Here we'll use yellow, red, and blue beads.

## SUPPLIES

- glass or plastic beads in yellow, red, and blue
- 3 feet (1 meter) of thin wire
- needle-nose pliers or old scissors

**1** Take two red beads and thread them halfway down your wire. Bend the wire on both sides of the red beads.

**2** Thread two yellow beads on one side of the wire so they form a second row above the red beads. Push the other wire end through these two yellow beads. This second wire end should go through the beads in the opposite direction from the first wire end. You should have one wire coming through each side. Bend each end of the wire.

**3** Now add two blue beads on one side of the wire. Repeat the rest of step two. Make sure you keep your wire tight while you are adding beads. There should be no loops or bumps of wire at the end of each bead row. Use the pliers to help you.

**4** Continue adding bead rows until your bracelet can circle around the widest part of your hand. Don't just measure your wrist, or you'll never be able to slip the bracelet over your hand to put it on!

**5** To finish the bracelet, push both ends of the wire through the first line of red beads, then through the next row of yellow beads. Cut the wire ends as close to the beads as possible so that they don't scratch you. Slip on your bracelet and show off your artwork!

The colors in Zulu beadwork can have double meanings. Black shows the happiness of marriage or the sadness of death. Pink symbolizes wealth, but also laziness. Red beads speak of love and emotion, but also of anger and impatience. The only beads without a double meaning are white. These beads represent love and purity.

### Chapter 11

# MUSIC

**M**usic is everywhere in Africa. Farmers sing songs while hoeing the soil. Women sing as they grind grain into flour. Children play singing and clapping games. Instead of listening alone to the latest iPod downloads, African people enjoy singing together at home and dancing with neighbors. At religious ceremonies, they gather together with song, dance, and instruments. African music often follows a call-and-response format. A leader will sing the verse, then others will join in the chorus. In this way, the community shares the music.

## The Significance of Music

While music can break up the working day, it can also have religious and ceremonial uses. Music is an important part of the traditions around birth, marriage, and death. Women sing sacred songs during a girl's initiation, or during childbirth. Music is present in ceremonies and rituals. Men perform hunting songs.

Every day, Maasai herders create and sing songs about herding and working in the village.

## WORDS TO KNOW

**spiritual:** about sacred things, religion, or the spirit world.

**missionary:** somebody doing church work in another country.

**percussion:** an instrument that one strikes to make a sound or tone.

For many Africans, music is **spiritual**. Some believe music links them to the spiritual world. For example, in the central African rainforest, the Baka people believe that bad things happen when the spirit of the rainforest has gone to sleep. They use music and song to wake the forest. In other parts of Africa, church **missionaries** have influenced spiritual music. In South African towns, songs of praise, hymns, and gospel-style music are common.

The melodies in African music are usually short and simple. Musicians often repeat the same melody many times. Several voices may sing different melodies at the same time.

The singers may also sing in a round style: each person sings the same melody, but they start at different times. As they perform, the singers and musicians often improvise or change the music. In this way, two performances of a song are rarely the same.

## Rhythm and Drums

More than melody, African music is about the rhythm. Drums are one of the most popular musical instruments in Africa. They can be small, simple hand drums or enormous, elaborately carved festival drums. Drums and other **percussion** instruments like shakers and bells layer over each other to create complex interlocking rhythm patterns.

### WORDS TO KNOW

**resonate:** to amplify or make louder through air vibrations.

**kora:** a harp-like instrument popular in West Africa.

Musicians usually carve drums out of wood and stretch a piece of animal skin across the top. Each type of drum has its own special use. In Ghana, the gankogui drum sets the beat to keep the musicians together. The donno, or talking, drum sends special messages when the drummer changes its notes and sound.

Most drummers use their hands to play the drum. Other drums are played with sticks. The drummer bounces his hand off the drum, causing it to **resonate**. A skilled drummer can make different sounds from the drum by striking it in different places or changing his hand positions.

Drums play an important role in many villages. They are used in healing, initiation, and naming ceremonies. Drums beat at warrior rituals and wedding celebrations. Village harvest and rain festivals feature drum music. Drums are even used to call people in the village. Different drum sounds let villagers know when it is time for work, when someone is in trouble, or even when it is time to worship.

For the Bagana people in the Great Lakes region of Africa, drums are a symbol of power. Each clan has its own type of drum and its own distinctive drum beat. The Bagana use their drums to signal from one clan to another. The size of the drum reflects the status of its owner. The most important drum in the clan belongs to the kabaka, or Baganda king.

African kings and chiefs often had special musicians in their court. They created songs of praise in the king's honor.

# The Instruments

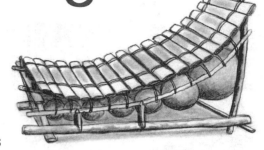

African music features many other percussion and rhythm instruments. The beat of the San people's trance dance is created by clapping and slapping the body, foot stamping, and dancing with rattles around the ankles. There are also shaking instruments, such as the axatse. These are hollowed-out gourds covered with a net strung with beads or seeds. People hold the axatse in one hand and beat it against the palm of the other hand.

## One of the simplest percussion instruments is the human body!

Balafons are like xylophones and are common in regions that have hardwood trees. The musician strings wooden bars together on a frame. Small gourds tied underneath the frame resonate the sound. The musician strikes the bars with a padded stick. Bells, or double bells, can be struck with sticks or rocks in a rhythmic pattern.

The West African Mande people of Mali are famous for an instrument called the **kora**. The kora is made from a large calabash gourd cut in half, covered with cow skin. It has a notched bridge like a guitar and a long neck with 21 leather strings attached to a rosewood pole. Kora players pluck the strings with their thumbs and index fingers.

## THUMB PIANOS

All over Africa, people play thumb pianos. They are called mbiras, kalimbas, or sansas. It can be made from simple cigar boxes or elaborately decorated metal boxes. The hollow box acts as a resonator to amplify, or make the sound louder.

Metal or bamboo keys attach to the top of the box. Longer keys have lower pitches and shorter keys have higher pitches. Simple thumb pianos may have only a few keys, or as many as 30 keys. The musician holds it in both hands and plucks the keys with his or her thumbs and fingers.

# African Music Today

Today, traditional African music is still heard, although less frequently. With more people moving to cities and western culture more widespread, new forms of music have emerged. Many of these styles combine traditional African music with Western elements.

One such style, **highlife**, has become a popular dance music across Africa and in Europe. It mixes the style of European brass bands and church hymns with West African traditional dance rhythms. This music is called highlife because it is used when dressing up and going out to dance in the city. Modern guitar bands and party bands play highlife music for dancing.

Some popular music styles in America can trace their roots to Africa. Enslaved people arriving in America brought music with them. Many of the sounds and rhythms from African music formed the basis of American jazz, blues, and rock.

**WORDS TO KNOW**

**highlife:** world music that combines African and European musical styles.

## THE LION OF ZIMBABWE

Musician Thomas Mapfumo, also known as the Lion of Zimbabwe, is that country's most famous musician. His music combines traditional Shona mbira music with western instruments like electric guitars, horns, and drums. His songs in the 1970s often spoke about the struggle for independence from the white government. This style of music became known as chimurenga, after the Shona word for struggle.

When Mapfumo released a song called "Hokoyo!" or "Watch out!" the government banned the record on the radio and put him in prison. This resulted in large demonstrations and three months later they released him. In 1980 the Zimbabwe people finally gained independence. Mapfumo continues to create music and perform worldwide with his band, Blacks Unlimited. Many of his songs are political and talk about poverty and other problems in Zimbabwe.

# MAKE YOUR OWN
## African Drum

**1** Have an adult help you use a can opener to cut the bottom off your can. Now you will have tube with two open ends. Use tape to cover any rough edges.

**2** Wrap the paper around the coffee can. Mark with a pencil where the top and bottom edges are and where the paper meets. Use those marks to trim the paper with your scissors so it fits tightly around the can.

**3** Lay the paper flat to color or paint it. Use colors, patterns, and designs. Be creative! You might want to tape or glue strips or shapes of different colors to decorate your drum. You can glue on small beads, hard pasta shapes, pebbles, seeds, or other decorative items. When you've finished decorating and the paint is dry, wrap the paper around the can, and fasten with tape.

**4** To make your drum's skin, you have two options. If your can came with a plastic lid, put that on the top and you're done! If not, use a heavy plastic garbage bag or liner to make your lid. First, place your can on the plastic bag and trace a circle that is about 2 inches bigger than your can. Cut out the circle. Smooth it over the top of the can and use a rubber band to hold it in place.

## SUPPLIES

- empty, clean coffee can with plastic lid
- can opener
- tape
- white paper or colored construction paper
- pencil
- scissors
- paint, brushes, markers, crayons, or colored pencils
- small beads, pebbles, seeds, buttons
- glue
- heavy plastic garbage bag or liner
- rubber band
- thin strong string

**5** Cut a piece of string long enough to wrap around the can and still have a few extra inches. Tie it securely around the top of the drum, near the rubber band. Knot in place.

**6** Now it's time to play your drum. How you hit the drum determines the type of sound you make. To make an open sound, hit the edge of your drum with a flat hand. To make a cupped sound, cup your hand when you strike the drum. A closed sound comes from placing one hand on the drum skin and then striking it with the other hand.

# MAKE YOUR OWN
## African Rain stick

African people traditionally make their own instruments out of things that are locally available. Bamboo and reeds can be made into wind instruments, such as flutes. Elephant tusks or animal horns make great trumpets. Wood, gourds, and animal fibers can become stringed instruments like musical bows, lutes, and lyres.

The musical bow is a simple homemade instrument. A single piece of string stretches across a curved piece of wood to form the bow. The bow's player usually plucks the string with his tongue and allows his mouth to resonate the sound.

Some instruments, like the rain stick, copy the sounds of nature. Usually it is made from a hollow tree trunk filled with seeds, pebbles, and shells. The musician tips the rain stick slowly so that the seeds and pebbles inside fall through the tube, sounding like a soft summer rain.

## SUPPLIES

- poster tube with plastic end cap to seal
- decorating supplies such as markers, paint, construction paper
- scissors
- glue or tape
- tin foil
- rice, dried beans, or seeds

**1** Decorate your poster cylinder using markers, paint, or construction paper. Cut out shapes and glue them on your rainstick. You might want to even decorate the cylinder using adinkra stamps!

**2** Cut a piece of tin foil three times the length of the poster tube. Roll it up tightly along its length, then coil it so that it is like a stretched out spring the length of the poster tube. Place the coil in the tube.

**3** Fill one-tenth of the tube with rice, beans, and seeds. The items you choose will give different sounds and textures to your rain stick. Seal the rain stick's open end with your plastic cap.

**4** Slowly tilt the rain stick and listen to the seeds inside fall to the other end. Experiment with your speed and see how the sound changes.

Ethiopian music is known more for its sad-sounding music than driving drum beats. It features the sounds of harps, lyres, reed flutes, and single voices in song.

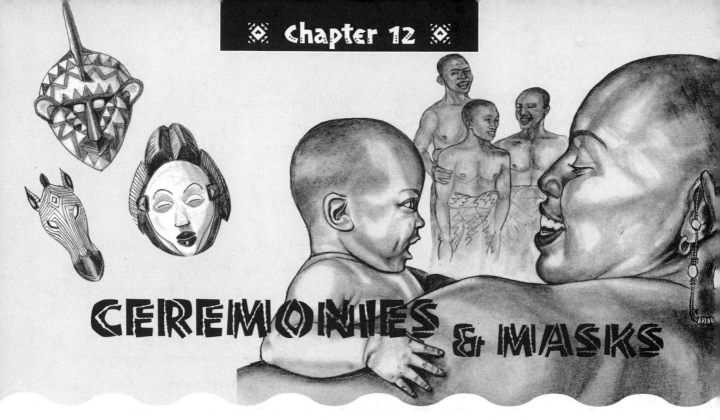

### Chapter 12

# CEREMONIES & MASKS

**A**ll over Africa, ceremonies and rituals are an important part of life. A ceremony or ritual is a set of special behaviors repeated at special times. For example, in the United States, Thanksgiving dinner is a seasonal ritual. In Africa, a seasonal ceremony might ask for a good rain or harvest.

## Coming of Age Ceremonies

Most Africans have special rituals or ceremonies when important changes happen in a person's life. These are called **rites of passage** or coming of age ceremonies. A person marks their change of status by changing their appearance during the ceremony. Shaving hair and wearing different clothes are ways to show change.

One of the first rites of passage occurs when a child is born. The Maasai shave the heads of both the mother and baby during a baby-naming ceremony. This shows how both mother and child are entering a new phase of life. The baby, its mother and father, and three elders then gather in the family hut. The elders pronounce the baby's name and say "May that name dwell in you."

## WORDS TO KNOW

**rites of passage:** special ceremonies or rituals when a person reaches certain milestones in life.

**initiation:** ceremony when a person leaves childhood to become an adult in the community.

**Initiation** is one of the most important and most common rites of passage in Africa. Initiation ceremonies mark the time when a person becomes an adult. They also prepare the person for their new role as adults.

In many societies, the young people leave the community for a period of time. They may enter a sacred house or place where elders teach skills they will need as adults in the community. Afterward the initiates often parade around to celebrate their new roles as adults.

## Boys and girls have separate initiations.

For Krobo girls in eastern Ghana, the Dipo initiation rituals are centuries old. The girls enter a ritual house where they exchange their childhood clothes for a beaded belt with a long red cloth. The girls shave their heads except for small tuft of hair in the back.

Over three weeks, women called ritual mothers teach the girls food preparation, grooming, art, and dances. Then the girls replace their red cloths with white ones and walk to a special grove of trees near the village.

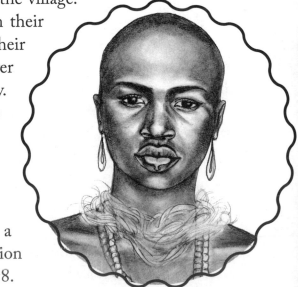

Along the walk, the girls carry a leaf between their lips. Their silence allows them to reflect on their new roles as women. Village priestesses lower them on a sacred stone for a final ceremony. Afterwards the ritual mothers carry the girls back to the village on their backs. The girls decorate themselves with headdresses and beads for the Outdooring ceremony, where the girls are presented to the community as women.

For African boys, initiation often involves a difficult or painful task. A Maasai boy's initiation usually occurs between the ages of 14 and 18.

# WEDDING CELEBRATIONS

African weddings are often a series of ceremonies. They can be as short as one day or as long as a week. Sometimes, huge wedding ceremonies marry many couples at the same time. The wedding ceremonies often separate the bride and groom and their guests. Some weddings place the bride and groom in isolation, so the ceremonies take place without them. In Islamic societies, the bride and groom may not see each other until the wedding night. While the details vary from ethnic group to ethnic group, African weddings are usually celebrations with lots of feasting, dancing, and animal sacrifices. The social celebrations help the two families form a bond.

At dawn, the boy splashes himself with cold water to numb his body. His friends hurl insults at him to toughen him up and build his courage for the ordeal ahead. The boy must prove his bravery. A painful experience bonds boys of the same age group. Together, they wear black clothing and elaborate headdresses for a few weeks to show their status as new initiates.

Other male initiation rituals, like the Hamar "Jumping of the Bull" in Ethiopia, are a physical challenge. In this ritual, a Hamar teen leaps over the backs of 20 to 40 bulls to prove he is a man. In West Africa, Bassari initiates fight a fierce masked spirit. Surviving the fight is a sign that the initiate will be brave enough to face life as a man.

## Funerals

Funeral rites are some of the largest village ceremonies. There are many superstitions around death in Africa. Some people believe that death opens a door to the spirit world. Until the dead person's spirit moves through this door, it disrupts the entire community. Funeral ceremonies help the dead person's spirit make a successful transition.

The Dogon people of Mali hold funerals in three parts. First, they wrap the body in cloth and lift it up to a special burial place in the cliffs. A year later, the Nyu Yama ceremony marks the person's death with song, dance, and animal sacrifice. A large funeral called the Dama, held every 12 years, honors everyone who has died since the last ceremony. Hundreds of masked dancers perform a series of dances to please the dead. They help the spirits journey to the world of their ancestors.

# Seasonal Ceremonies

Like all ancient societies, the African people have had to understand nature and the seasons to survive. Many African cultures believe nature has spirits that control the world around them. Seasonal ceremonies ask for the protection of the spirit world against disasters such as drought and flood. The Bobo in Burkina Faso and Mali hold elaborate masked rituals to ask for permission to plant and harvest crops. They believe nature will send a terrible drought to their lands without these ceremonies.

# Masks

In west and central Africa, masks play an important part of many rituals, ceremonies, and social events. Masks have a strong visual impact.

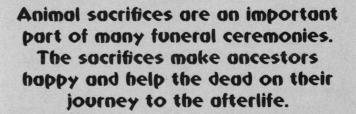

Animal sacrifices are an important part of many funeral ceremonies. The sacrifices make ancestors happy and help the dead on their journey to the afterlife.

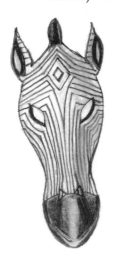

They are used to discipline, educate, inform, and entertain people. Masks come in thousands of shapes and sizes and represent ancestors or nature spirits. Some masks fit over the face, while other rest on top of the dancer's head.

Craftsmen carve intricate wooden masks out of ebony, mahogany, or teak. They stain or color the masks with vegetable dyes. Each color has meaning. The craftsman might use beads to decorate the mask or other materials such as metal, fabric, leather, and grasses.

# TALKING TO ANCESTORS

In Africa, ancestors are a valuable link between the community and the spirit world. Not everyone can become an ancestor. First they must live a long, good life in the human world before joining the ancestors in the spirit world. Sometimes the head of the family communicates with the ancestors to get their advice. Other societies have special soothsayers, diviners, priests, or priestesses who approach the ancestors. The communicators use many different methods to speak to the ancestors, such as reading sacred items or listening to a special gourd.

A ceremonial mask holds a place of great respect in African communities. Some masks pass down from generation to generation in the village. These masks may hang in a place of honor in a special village room. Other masks are destroyed at the end of the ceremony.

For seasonal ceremonies, masks are often in the form of animals. These represent the spirits of nature who link man and the creator god. For funeral ceremonies, masks represent spirits, myths, and ancestors. These spirits come to life during the funeral **masquerade** to help the dead pass over into the next world. They also offer comfort to the grieving family. A Dogon Dama funeral features over 65 different masks.

A masquerade is performed for seasonal changes or major life events. These dances are usually noisy and exciting with lots of drumming and shaking of

## WORDS TO KNOW

**masquerade:** a masked dance performed at ceremonies and rituals.

leg rattles. People believe masquerades summon the spirits to help crops grow, transform young people into adults, and lead the dead to the afterlife.

A masked dancer will wear a colorful costume and use movements like those of his mask's character. When wearing a mask, the dancer's individual identity disappears. He is not acting—he has become the spirit of the mask. The dancer is transformed into a link between the group and the spiritual world.

Seasonal ceremonies ask for blessings from nature's spirits before planting, harvesting, hunting, and moving herds of livestock. Some seasonal ceremonies celebrate a successful hunt or harvest.

Masked dancers are almost always men. In some villages, the masked men are part of a secret society. Members of the secret societies are initiated at a young age and trained in mask skills. Some of these secret societies even teach their members a secret language so they can talk without outsiders understanding them. In some villages, these societies also enforce the community's laws.

# Today

Western influences have changed traditional African ceremonies and masquerades. With the spread of Christianity and Islam, many Africans practice both new and traditional religions. They may go to Sunday church and then attend a traditional ceremony. Craftsmen may make masks for tourists instead of ceremonies and rituals. Unfortunately, as more people move to African cities and lose their connection to their villages, ceremonies and masked dances become less common.

# THE FANG'S NGIL SOCIETY

In Gabon's Fang people, the Ngil society was a secret group of men with great power. They enforced the community's laws. A terrifying sight, they would arrive in the middle of the night with torches to take a person away for punishment. The members of Ngil used fearsome masks to frighten the people in their village. The masks had eyes like slits and a huge bulging forehead. The Fang people believed these masks represented the spirits of the dead. The spirits protected the mask's wearer from evil and poisons. The Ngil society was disbanded around a hundred years ago.

# MAKE YOUR OWN
## Kikuyu Initiation Shield

The Kikuyu people are the largest ethnic group in Kenya. Young men wear special initiation shields before becoming junior warriors. The shields are carved from wood and are often passed down within families and repainted for each initiation. The shields also have an "eye" cut out of the center.

**1** Draw your shield using a pencil on the cardboard. The shield shape should be a large oval with pointed ends at the top and bottom. Cut it out with heavy duty scissors. Draw a small eye in the center of the shield. The eye should mirror the shape of the shield—a small oval with a pointed top and bottom. Carefully punch the scissors through the eye and then cut it out. Save your scrap pieces of cardboard.

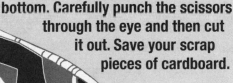

## SUPPLIES

- large piece of cardboard or heavy poster board
- pencil
- scissors
- brown, black, and red paint
- paint brushes
- tape or stapler

**2** Paint the entire shield brown. When the paint is dry, draw a line down the center of the shield, passing through the eye. Draw a design pattern on your shield, making the two halves mirror images of each other.

**3** Use black and red paint to color your design on the shield. Also paint the center dividing line.

**4** Cut a rectangular piece from your scrap cardboard, measuring about 2 inches (5 centimeters) wide by 7 inches (18 centimeters) long. Once the shield's paint is dry, tape or staple the rectangle at each end to the back of the shield to make a handle for carrying the shield.

# MAKE YOUR OWN
## Ceremonial Mask

Masks are an important part of African ceremonies. Here's your chance to make one for yourself. Cover a work surface with newspaper. This project can be messy!

**1** Rip sheets of newspaper into small, 1-inch (2-centimeter) pieces. Blow up the balloon and knot the end. Make your balloon about the size you want your mask to be.

**2** Mix glue and warm water in a large bowl. They should be in equal parts. If you put in 4 ounces (120 milliliters) of glue, you'll need to measure out 4 ounces of water.

**3** Soak the newspaper pieces in the water-glue mixture for 3 minutes. Layer the pieces of newspaper on one side of the balloon. You don't want to cover the entire balloon, just enough to make a mask-like shape. After the first layer is complete, let it dry for 10 minutes. Repeat with a second layer of newspaper, letting each layer dry in between.

**4** Quickly dip a sheet of tissue paper into the water-glue mixture. Scrunch the wet tissue and use it to shape a face on your mask. Form a nose, lips, and eyebrows. Once you've completed the face, add another layer of newspaper over it.

## SUPPLIES

- newspaper
- balloon
- large bowl
- water-soluble glue
- warm water and measuring cup
- tissue paper
- white paper
- scissors
- paint and brushes

**5** Rip pieces of white paper, soak in the water-glue mixture and use as the final layer for your mask. Now let it dry for 24 hours.

**6** Once your mask is completely dry, let the air out of the balloon. Have an adult help you cut out eye and mouth holes. Use scissors to trim the mask's edges into the shape you want.

**7** Paint the mask using your own designs. Paint lines, squiggles, dots, and shapes in any pattern you want.

### Chapter 13

# LANGUAGE & STORYTELLING

**H**ow many languages do you speak? Many American kids only speak English. If your grandparents or parents came from another county, though, you might speak a second language at home like Spanish or Chinese.

Most African kids know several languages! A typical Kenyan boy speaks three or four. At home, he'll talk in his local language with the family. At school, he and the class use English. With friends, the boy might switch to **Swahili**, a common language that Africans from different ethnic groups understand. On the streets, he might speak Sheng, a slang-based mixture of several languages.

There are more than 1,000 different languages in Africa, more than any other continent.

# Why So Many Languages?

It is not surprising that African kids use so many languages. Almost all African countries were **colonized** by Europeans at some point in their history. Most have one or more European languages like French, Portuguese, or English as an official language, along with the native African languages. South Africa has 11 official languages! Compare that to the United States, where there's only one.

All of the African languages can be grouped into four language families. Languages in the same family might share some vocabulary and grammar.

The Khoisan family of languages are the "click" languages. These are some of the most distinctive languages in Africa. They are used by ethnic groups like the San, Zulu, and Xhosa in southern Africa. These languages have many consonants and are spoken by clicking the tongue off the roof of the mouth. A speaker can make different click sounds by moving his tongue to different parts inside the mouth.

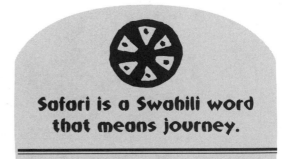

**Safari is a Swahili word that means journey.**

## WORDS TO KNOW

**Swahili:** a common language used by several ethnic groups in Africa.

**colonize:** when a country settles another country and takes over.

**dialects:** variations of the same language that uses different sounds and words.

**oral literature:** spoken stories.

**communal:** shared by everyone in a group or community.

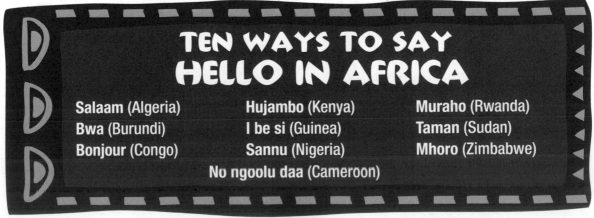

## TEN WAYS TO SAY HELLO IN AFRICA

| | | |
|---|---|---|
| **Salaam** (Algeria) | **Hujambo** (Kenya) | **Muraho** (Rwanda) |
| **Bwa** (Burundi) | **I be si** (Guinea) | **Taman** (Sudan) |
| **Bonjour** (Congo) | **Sannu** (Nigeria) | **Mhoro** (Zimbabwe) |
| | **No ngoolu daa** (Cameroon) | |

To make things even more complicated, some people who speak the same language use different **dialects**. Listening to different dialects is like listening to a person from New York and a person from Australia. You can understand them both, but some words or sounds may be different.

**Some Khoisan words may use more than 15 different click sounds.**

# African storytelling

Most African languages were not written down until recently. So African people have used **oral literature** to record their history, culture, customs, and social values. Through repetition, their stories, songs, proverbs, and folktales were passed from generation to generation. A story's survival depended on the memories of the new generation. Although the introduction of writing has eroded some of Africa's oral traditions, many still exist today.

**Traditional African tales constantly change and adapt to current happenings in the community.**

African oral literature is a **communal** activity. Like performers, storytellers must entertain their audience. They add music, dance, and song to their tales. They may act out parts of the tale with impersonations of characters or use masks and costumes. Each time storytellers perform, they may add new twists or elements.

The audience is an important part of the African storytelling experience. They may repeat certain phrases in a call-and-answer format with the storyteller, or join in the song or dance of the story. Depending on how the performer is doing, they may shout out praise or criticism during the tale.

The storyteller may be a respected elder or from a special group of people. In West Africa, for example, traditional storytellers and musicians are called **griots**. Good griots have great memories and can recite or sing long histories. Boys and girls become griots by first learning from their griot parents. Then they attend a formal school and learn from a master. Today, griots perform at ceremonies and parties, record CDs, and perform on television and radio.

African storytellers do more than just entertain. They teach about the world around them and the history of their people. Tales can show how to survive in nature or live within the community. Each ethnic group has its own set of stories and ways of telling them. Some types of stories, like creation **myths** and trickster tales, are common across Africa, even though the actual story may be different for each group.

**Creation myths generally try to explain the origins of things in the world.**

One Kenyan myth explains how elephants were created. A poor man wanted to grow rich. He took a potion from a magician and rubbed it on his wife's upper teeth. The teeth grew into ivory tusks, which the man sold for a lot of money. The greedy man tried to use the potion a second time. This time, his wife grew to an enormous size. Her skin turned grey and wrinkled and she ran off to live in the forest. This explains why elephants are as smart as people.

Trickster tales are some of the most common African stories. Usually, the trickster is an animal who acts and speaks like a human. Popular trickster characters are monkeys, rabbits, spiders, or tortoises. The trickster can be wise, foolish, funny, or lazy. He uses his creativity to outwit bigger and stronger animals.

## WORDS TO KNOW

**griot:** a person in Western Africa who remembers oral histories and entertains with stories, songs, poems, and dances.

**myth:** a legendary story that often features a god or spirit that explains a practice, rite, or happening in nature.

**dilemma:** a difficult situation or problem.

In one central African tale, a hare plans to get married, but is too lazy to set up a home for his future wife. First, he asks a hippopotamus to hold one end of a long rope. Next, he convinces the elephant to hold the rope's other end. The hippo and the elephant cannot see each other and begin a powerful tug-of-war. The rope's back and forth motion brings down many trees and clears undergrowth. The wily hare moves with his wife onto the land the hippo and elephant unknowingly prepared for him.

Many characters in African tales are animals like elephants, giraffes, birds, and crocodiles who act like humans. They show greed, jealousy, and honesty. These stories teach the members of the community how to behave and get along with each other. Also, the surroundings of the tales can teach the people about nature. Details about the dry and rainy seasons or the behavior of plants and animals teach people important survival skills.

Another type of African tale is the **dilemma** story. These stories have unresolved or puzzling endings. They encourage the audience or people in the group to talk about the story and solve the ending together.

# WOLE SOYINKA

In 1986 Wole Soyinka became the first African to win the Nobel Prize in Literature. A Nigerian born in 1934, Soyinka is a man of many talents. He has published 20 works of poetry, novels, and plays. Educated in Africa and England, his plays blend European traditions with African theater's style of dance, music, and action. Much of his writing uses the mythology of his ancesters, the Yoruba, which features Ogun, the god of iron and war.

Soyinka has been imprisoned for speaking out publicly about the political issues of his country. At times, his views put Soyinka at risk. He had to leave Nigeria during the 1990s for this reason.

# A STORY FROM LIBERIA

Many African folktales prepare young people for life. The tales teach lessons about behavior and the roles of men and women. Here's a famous story from Liberia.

A woman with a baby strapped to her back walked through the forest with a man. The path was rough and overgrown with vines and shrubs. They were very hungry. As they emerged from the forest onto a grassy plain, they saw a herd of grazing cows. The man told the woman that she has the power to transform herself. He asked her to transform into a leopard and capture a cow for him to eat. The woman untied her baby and placed it on the ground. Hair grew from her neck and body. Her hands and feet turned into claws. In a few minutes, a wild leopard stood with fiery eyes before the man. He was so frightened that he climbed up a tree. When he had almost reached the top, he remembered the baby on the ground. But he was too afraid to come down and rescue the child.

When the leopard saw she had thoroughly frightened the man, she ran to the herd, captured a cow, and dragged it back to the foot of the tree. The man, still high in the tree, begged the leopard to transform back into a woman. Slowly, the hair and claws disappeared and the woman stood on the ground again. He refused to come down, however, until she tied the baby to her back. Then she told him, "Never ask a woman to do a man's work again."

In one Hausa story, a man ran away from his village. He took all of his property, a leopard, a goat, and a yam. When he reached the river, there was only one small canoe for crossing. He could only fit one piece of his property at a time in the canoe. If left alone, the goat would eat the yam and the leopard would eat the goat. How would he be able to get all of his property across the river safely?

After discussion, the tribe would conclude that the man should take the goat in the canoe first, then the yam. Leaving the yam on shore, he should bring the goat back with him to his original spot. Next, he should row the leopard across, leaving it with the yam. Finally, the man should return for the goat and row across the river one last time to join the leopard and the yam.

# MAKE YOUR OWN
## African Fable

Fables often feature animal characters who talk and act like humans. The story usually teaches a lesson or tries to explain the origin of something. Get your creative juices flowing and write your own African fable.

**1** Choose the characters in your fable. You can use animals, humans, or even spirits in the tale. Most animals use their word as a name, like Cat or Rabbit.

**2** Try to think of a moral for your story. You might want to teach your little brother to share, or your neighbor to speak nicely to others. Think about how your characters could demonstrate that moral in your story.

**3** Write freely. Keep it simple and don't worry about editing. Write like you are telling the story to a group of children. It shouldn't be long or complicated.

## SUPPLIES

- your imagination
- pencil
- paper

**4** Once your story is complete, think about elements to add to your storytelling performance. Are there places where the audience can repeat certain lines? Can you act out any of the characters? After practicing a few times, share your story with family and friends.

## AFRICAN PROVERBS

A proverb is a short saying that gives practical advice. It can teach common truths and values or illustrate basic rules of behavior. Here are some well-known African proverbs.

The elephant does not get tired of its tusks. Meaning: Carry your burdens without complaint.

A roaring lion kills no game. Meaning: You will not gain by sitting or talking. You must stand up and work for it.

Rain does not fall on one roof alone. Meaning: Everyone has trouble at some time in their life.

Restless feet may walk into a snake pit. Meaning: It is easy to get into trouble if you are not busy doing something.

Teeth do not see poverty. Meaning: Smile despite your problems.

Only a fool tests the depth of water with both feet. Meaning: Think about a situation before you jump into it.

# MAKE YOUR OWN
## Fon Story Banner

When a Fon king of Benin rose to the throne, he was expected to decorate a cloth with his achievements for a story banner. The banner's pictures told the story of a great battle or important events in the king's life. A special tailor made the banner's pictures with brightly colored cotton cloth. The tailor sewed the figures onto the banner background, which was usually black or white. Many banners featured a large, central figure surrounded by smaller figures. The size of the figures showed their importance. Some kings had themselves portrayed as a fierce animal like a lion.

At first, Fon story banners were only made for kings to display near thrones and during ceremonies. Over time, however, ordinary people displayed banners in their homes. The purpose of the banner remained the same—to show a person's achievements and strengths. Today, tourists can buy Fon story cloths.

## SUPPLIES

- several squares of colored felt
- marker
- scissors
- large piece of white or black felt
- glue

**2** Using a marker, draw your figures on the colored squares of felt. Cut out each felt figure. You can use extra pieces of felt to decorate your figures—creating eyes, mouths, stripes, etc.

**3** Arrange your story's pictures on the large piece of background felt. Move the pieces around and try them in different places on the banner until you are satisfied with the story. Glue the felt figures into place on the banner.

**1** Choose the story in your life you'd like to tell on your Fon banner. What characters and symbols will you need? What type of animal or figure will you use to represent yourself? Think about what things are important in your life. A piano player might want to draw music notes and a soccer player might want soccer balls on the banner.

### Chapter 14

# OVERCOMING CHALLENGES

**I**n its long history, the African continent and its people have faced many challenges. Nature, invaders, and even some African people themselves have threatened the rich and diverse way of life in Africa.

Through it all, the African people have proven their resilience. They have found ways to overcome challenges. Today, poverty, hunger, disease, and climate change threaten Africa. With the help of the world, Africa stands ready to tackle the future.

Ethiopia and Liberia are the only two African nations that were never colonized by Europe.

# Slavery

As in many other civilizations, for centuries **slavery** was practiced in some parts of Africa. People captured in wars were **enslaved**. Criminals or people unable to pay their debts were sometimes forced into slavery.

Outsiders also captured and enslaved Africans. Arab slave traders sent raiding parties to capture the biggest and strongest people. When the Portuguese arrived in the 1400s, they traded for African gold and other metals. Soon, they began capturing Africans. Local chiefs also willingly sold people. In return, the Europeans gave the Africans horses, weapons, and luxury goods from Europe.

As Europeans explored and settled the Americas, they grew sugar, tobacco, and cotton on **plantations** there. Sugar could be made into valuable rum. These plantations needed large numbers of workers to plant and work the fields. Slave labor was a cheap, plentiful solution.

**Tobacco Leaves**

Europeans traded Africans for sugar in the Americas, and then sold the sugar for cash in Europe. With the cash, they purchased guns to trade with African chiefs for more people. This was called the Triangle Trade Route because it formed a triangle between the Americas, Europe, and Africa.

Traders shipped over 9 million Africans to the Americas between 1451 and 1870. Millions more died during capture or on the passage across the Atlantic. Most were enslaved in the Caribbean and South America. A smaller number traveled to North America's plantations.

## WORDS TO KNOW

**slavery:** system based on owning people and forcing them to work.

**enslave:** to take someone and claim to own them.

**plantation:** a large farm or estate where crops are grown.

**abolish:** to do away with or end.

**Scramble for Africa:** period between 1885 and 1910 when Europe rushed to establish colonies in Africa.

African kingdoms like the Asante and Dahomey grew rich and powerful in the slave trade. They expanded their kingdoms with the guns they received. In raids on neighbors they captured more people to trade.

Public opinion helped to end the slave trade. A movement to **abolish** slavery began in the late 1700s. By the early 1800s, most European nations banned the slave trade. Later they abolished the use of slaves. The United States officially abolished slavery in 1865.

Olaudah Equiano was enslaved and taken to the Americas. Eventually, he bought his freedom and wrote about his experiences. His writings were read throughout the Americas and Europe. They played an important role in turning public opinion against slavery.

**Africans were not slaves. They were enslaved. Slavery is a condition placed on another person.**

The Atlantic slave trade had lasting effects on Africa. Millions of the strongest and brightest Africans were stolen from Africa, never to return again. The slave trade introduced deadly weapons and increased violence among ethnic groups. Many African economies were ruined when the slave trade ended. Ultimately, it made Europe richer and Africa poorer.

# Colonialism

In the late 1800s, Europeans began discovering Africa's gold, diamonds, and other valuable resources. European nations scrambled to claim land and build permanent settlements and forts. They ignored the rights of the African people who had been living there for thousands of years.

The period between 1885 and 1910 is known as the **Scramble for Africa**. In 25 years, European nations colonized most of Africa. They drew borders for the colonies without paying attention to the people already there. Some borders split ethnic groups. Other lines joined groups that had never been together before.

The colonies took advantage of African labor and grew rich off the continent's mineral resources.

At the time, European colonists saw themselves as the most advanced people in the world. They felt it was their duty to spread their values and beliefs. This attitude was used to excuse their actions. Christian missionaries built churches and encouraged Africans to abandon their religions and traditional way of life. Some aspects of African culture, like oral histories and nature skills, were lost forever.

**Many European nations had colonies in Africa, including Great Britain, France, Germany, Italy, Portugal, Spain, and Belgium.**

Colonization caused many problems. Africans got the worst, lowest-paying jobs. They were not free to choose their own rulers. In many places, they weren't allowed to own property or move around as they wanted. Families were broken up as the men traveled to work in European mining operations.

# Nationalism and Independence

After World War II, African **nationalism** grew quickly. Uprisings spread throughout Africa. Eventually, Europe granted the colonies independence. Ghana became the first **sub-Saharan** colony to become independent, in 1957.

Even after winning independence, it was not easy for African nations. Borders ignored ethnic groups. People within a country often had different cultures, languages, and traditions. Many felt loyalty to their ethnic group over their country. For many African countries, this feeling of separateness led to bloody civil wars.

## WORDS TO KNOW

**nationalism:** the desire for a nation's independence and advancement.

**sub-Sahara:** south of the Sahara Desert.

**corrupt:** guilty of dishonest behavior like lying, stealing, or bribing.

**apartheid:** a system that separated different people, giving privileges to whites.

**minority:** a small group.

**discriminate:** treat people unfairly based on their skin color, ethnic group, or religion.

**segregate:** to keep groups separate.

The colonial period left Africa with other challenges as well. At the time of independence only 10 percent of the people could read. Roads and railways were only good for exporting Africa's resources to Europe. There were few links between African countries for trade. Telephones within Africa were rare, making communication difficult.

Many African leaders believed they needed to be like Europe to succeed. They rushed to build transportation, schools, and manufacturing plants. They borrowed money to pay for these projects, more money than they could repay.

**Corrupt** officials stole some of this money. They completed projects in sloppy ways, like building a bridge with cheap steel, and kept the extra money. Citizens eventually demanded fairness and honesty from their government officials. Many African governments now have anti-corruption departments.

# Nelson Mandela & Apartheid

In 1948 a group came to power in South Africa that supported **apartheid**. Apartheid is a program that separates people based on the color of their skin. The word apartheid comes from an Afrikaans word that means separateness.

Under apartheid, a **minority** of South African whites **discriminated** against African blacks and people of other races. They made laws that required each person to carry a pass card that identified their race as white, black, or mixed descent. Whites and non-whites were not allowed to marry. Non-whites could not hold certain jobs or even enter white areas. Public services like schools, buses, and hospitals were **segregated**. The apartheid government passed laws that said where the races could live. The laws restricted blacks to areas called homelands.

Some Africans resisted these policies. Nelson Mandela, a member of the Tembu ethnic group, joined the African National Congress (ANC). He supported the idea of using military tactics to overthrow the apartheid government.

The white government of South Africa arrested Mandela and sentenced him to life in prison in 1964. Mandela became a symbol for the struggle against apartheid. Nations around the world **boycotted** South Africa and called for an end to apartheid. Citizens rioted and protested against apartheid.

Finally, in 1990 the South African president declared apartheid illegal. Nelson Mandela was released from prison. He continued to work for equality for all races in South Africa. In 1993 Mandela was awarded the Nobel Peace prize. In South Africa's 1994 free election, the people chose Nelson Mandela as their first non-white president.

**boycott:** refuse to have anything to do with something in protest.

**stigma:** shame or disgrace.

# The Future

Africa faces huge challenges. Violent civil wars continue to tear apart regions. African countries are some of the poorest in the world. According to a 2008 United Nations report, two-fifths of Africa's people live on less than $1 per day. Jobs are scarce in many areas and many young people can't find work. Four in ten African children are hungry or undernourished. These kids are more likely to get sick and die.

**Diseases pose serious health threats to Africa. In 2007, 75 percent of the world's people with AIDS/HIV lived in Africa. 90 percent of malaria deaths happened in Africa.**

Africa's climate is also changing. Less rain has led to drought. Crops suffer and herders spend more time looking for water and grass for their livestock. Many African countries are looking into ways to deal with these climate changes.

Some are building dams and irrigation systems to protect farm crops. Others are setting up local grain banks to store food for times of need.

Population growth has led to increased pollution and the overuse of natural resources like water and trees. When people are poor, they are more concerned with survival than environmental causes. They will cut down important rainforests in order to grow crops to feed their families.

Despite these serious challenges, the people of Africa remain strong and resilient. They have survived for thousands of years on the world's oldest continent. They have shown time after time how they can face and overcome challenges. This strength will help them create solutions for the future.

# AIDS IN AFRICA

The AIDS epidemic is one of the most serious challenges Africa faces today. Scientists believe the AIDS virus spread to humans from West African monkeys. **Stigma** surrounding AIDS prevented many people from talking openly about it. Religious leaders opposed public safety campaigns. Some governments even banned speaking about the disease in the press.

As a result, AIDS spread quickly across the African continent. More than 21 million people were living with AIDS/HIV in 2007. In areas with high rates of infection, like South Africa, 15 to 20 percent of adults have the deadly disease. Since the beginning of the epidemic, more than 15 million Africans have died. In 2007 alone, approximately 1.5 million people died of AIDS.

Recently, several companies have agreed to cut the prices of AIDS drugs to make them more affordable to Africans. In addition, the World Health Organization has worked to get the drugs into the people's hands. Because of these strategies, more Africans today receive treatment than ever before.

The impact of AIDS on Africa is devastating. More than 11 million children have been orphaned. Poverty and hunger have become problems in AIDS-stricken communities. There are fewer adults to work and produce food.

There are hopeful signs. Countries like Kenya and Zimbabwe have launched prevention campaigns and have seen AIDS decline in recent years. Their blueprint for success may help the rest of Africa fight this deadly disease.

# How Can You Help?

Want to help kids in Africa? There are lots of ways you can use your creativity to make a difference in an African child's life. One dollar in America will buy a pack of gum or let you play a couple of video games. In Africa, that same dollar will pay for a doctor's visit, buy malaria cures for three people, feed a child three meals, or buy a set of clothes for a small child. Through Nothing but Nets (www.nothingbutnets.net), you can buy a life-saving malaria net for an African family for only $10.

There a lots of ways you can raise money for people in Africa. Use some of the following ideas or come up with your own.

- Ask relatives to donate money instead of giving you birthday gifts.
- Design and sell T-shirts.
- Hold a car wash, bake sale, or garage sale.
- Organize a dance marathon or talent show and get some sponsors.

To make sure your money is going to reputable charities, make sure you ask an adult to help you donate your money. To compare charities, you might want to visit the Charity Navigator website (www.charitynavigator.org), which evaluates and rates charities around the world.

Another way to help an African child directly is to organize a book drive. Education and reading give children a window to the world and a helping step out of poverty. Check out Books for Africa (www.booksforafrica.org) for book guidelines and information on where to send the books you've collected.

# GLOSSARY

**abolish:** to do away with or end.

**adapt:** changes a plant or animal makes to survive in new or different conditions.

**adornment:** jewelry or other decorations to make the body beautiful.

**age set:** a group of people born in the same year or group of years.

**alloy:** mixture of metals.

**ancestor:** people from your family or country that lived before you.

**apartheid:** a system that separated different people, giving privileges to whites.

**archaeologist:** a scientist who studies ancient people and their cultures.

**architecture:** the art and science of designing and constructing buildings.

**artifact:** a simple object like a tool or piece of pottery from a culture.

**atmosphere:** the gases that surround the earth.

**BCE/CE:** Before Common Era, leading up to the year 0, and Common Era, after 0.

**biodiverse:** a lot of different forms of life in an area.

**blood diamond:** diamonds sold to pay for war.

**boycott:** refuse to have anything to do with something in protest.

**brass:** an alloy of copper and zinc.

**burnish:** polish with friction to make smooth and bright.

**calabash:** a bottle-shaped gourd.

**caldera:** a large depression in the earth caused by a volcano's collapse.

**carbon dioxide:** a gas created when animals breathe, plants and animals rot, or something is burned.

**carat:** the weight of a diamond. One carat equals one-fifth gram.

**carnivore:** an animal that eats meat.

**chrysomelid:** a small, brightly colored beetle.

**civil war:** war between groups in a country.

**civilization:** a highly developed society.

**climate:** average weather patterns in an area over a period of many years.

**coiling:** winding in a ring shape.

**colonization:** when one country settles in another country.

**colonize:** when a country settles another country and takes over.

**communal:** shared by everyone in a group or community.

**conduct:** to serve as a channel for heat or electricity.

**corrupt:** guilty of dishonest behavior like lying, stealing, or bribing.

**courtyard:** an open space surrounded by walls or buildings.

**crops:** plants grown for food and other uses.

**deforestation:** clearing forests to use the land for other purposes.

**delta:** area at the mouth of a river.

**desert:** a landscape or region with very little precipitation (rain or snow).

**dialects:** variations of the same language that uses different sounds and words.

**dilemma:** a difficult situation or problem.

**discriminate:** treat people unfairly based on their skin color, ethnic group, or religion.

**diverse:** when there are many different kinds of something.

**drought:** a long period of extremely dry weather.

**dung:** animal waste.

**elders:** older and wiser people.

**Enkai:** god of the Maasai people.

**enkang:** a Maasai village.

**enslave:** to take someone and claim to own them.

**erosion:** slowly wear away.

**ethnic group:** a group with common ancestors sharing customs, languages, and beliefs.

**extinct:** when an entire species dies.

**fertile:** rich in nutrients and good for growing plants.

**fertility:** able to have children.

**fossil:** the remains of an ancient plant or animal preserved in rock.

**fufu:** thick porridge or paste made with yams, cassava, or grains.

**galimoto:** a homemade push toy.

**gemsbok:** large antelope.

**geologist:** a scientist who studies rocks, minerals, and the structure of the earth.

**griot:** a person in Western Africa who remembers oral histories and entertains with stories, songs, poems, and dances.

**haggle:** bargain for a lower price.

**herd:** gather, keep, or drive sheep, cattle or other animals.

**hieroglyphics:** ancient Egypt's earliest form of writing.

**highlife:** world music that combines African and European musical styles.

**initiation:** ceremony when a person leaves childhood to become an adult in the community.

**insulate:** keep hot or cool air inside.

**kente cloth:** a type of fabric made of interwoven cloth strips.

**keratin:** a tough protein substance found in hair, fingernails, horns, and hooves.

# GLOSSARY

**kora:** a harp-like instrument popular in West Africa.

**larva:** an insect in its wingless, wormlike stage of life.

**magma:** melted rock in the earth's crust.

**manyatta:** Maasai warrior village separate from the main village.

**masquerade:** a masked dance.

**matriarchal:** group headed by a female leader.

**migrant worker:** a person who moves from place to place to find work.

**mine:** to remove minerals from the ground.

**minerals:** the crystal structures that make rocks.

**minority:** a small group.

**missionary:** somebody doing church work in another country.

**monarchy:** supreme power held by a single person like a king or queen.

**mortar:** a bowl used for grinding or crushing grain.

**myth:** a legendary story that often features a god or spirit that explains a practice, rite, or happening in nature.

**nationalism:** the desire for a nation's independence and advancement.

**nomadic:** a life of moving around.

**nutrients:** the substances in food and soil that animals and plants need to grow.

**oba:** king of the ancient Benin civilization.

**oral literature:** spoken stories.

**ore:** a metal-bearing rock.

**percussion:** an instrument that one strikes to make a sound or tone.

**pestle:** a long stick or pole used to pound or grind grain in a mortar bowl.

**pharaoh:** an ancient Egyptian king.

**plantation:** a large farm or estate where crops are grown.

**predator:** an animal that hunts other animals for food.

**prestigious:** held in high regard.

**prey:** an animal hunted for food.

**pride:** group of lions.

**primates:** a grouping of animals that includes apes, monkeys, and humans.

**prospector:** a person who explores an area for mineral deposits like gold or diamonds.

**pupae:** an insect in its cocoon where it changes from a larva to an adult.

**pyramids:** monuments that hold the tomb of ancient Egyptian pharaohs.

**refine:** to make pure.

**resonate:** to amplify or make louder through air vibrations.

**rifting:** to split open or break apart.

**rites of passage:** special ceremonies or rituals when a person reaches certain milestones in life.

**ritual:** a set of actions performed the same way each time.

**river basin:** a portion of land drained by a river.

**safari:** a journey to explore, most often used to describe a trip to explore Africa.

**Sahara Desert:** the world's largest desert, located in northern Africa.

**savanna:** wide open, grassy area.

**scarification:** the act of scarring or scratching the body.

**Scramble for Africa:** period between 1885 and 1910 when Europe rushed to establish colonies in Africa.

**scribes:** ancient Egyptians who read and wrote hieroglyphs.

**sediment:** dirt and other material deposited by water.

**segregate:** to keep groups separate.

**shantytown:** settlements of shacks.

**shuka:** red robe worn by Maasai warriors.

**slag:** waste material from smelting iron.

**slavery:** system based on owning people and forcing them to work.

**smelting:** to melt ore to separate the metal from a rock.

**snare:** an animal trap.

**sorghum:** a type of grain grass common in Africa.

**species:** a type of animal or plant.

**spiritual:** about sacred things, religion, or the spirit world.

**stigma:** shame or disgrace.

**sub-Sahara:** south of the Sahara Desert.

**Swahili:** a common language used by several ethnic groups in Africa.

**thatch:** to cover a roof with a material such as long grasses, straw, or leaves.

**track:** to follow.

**tribute:** payment made by one ruler or state to another as a sign of submission.

**tunic:** a gown-like outer garment, with or without sleeves.

**tuyeres:** pipes placed into a furnace where air enters.

**United Nations:** an international organization that promotes world peace, global cooperation, and human rights.

**wildebeest:** a member of the antelope family that lives in the grassy plains and open woodlands of central, eastern and southern Africa.

**wildlife:** wild animals and birds.

# INDEX

## A

activities (Make Your Own...)
  Adinkra Stamping, 38
  African Drum, 93
  African Fable, 109
  African Family Compound, 64
  African Fufu, 73
  African Rain Stick, 94
  African Savanna, 30
  Basket, 74
  Beaded Bracelet, 87
  Ceremonial Mask, 102
  Dogon Antelope Mask, 47
  Fon Story Banner, 110
  Golden Amulet, 21
  Horned Staff, 46
  Kente Strip Weaving, 86
  Kikuyu Initiation Shield, 101
  Leopard Mask, 31
  Maasai Beaded Necklace, 58
  Mancala Game, 78–79
  Ndebele House Painting, 63
  Rainforest Vine, 12
  Rock Paintings, 57
  Senufo Mud Painting, 48
  Soccer Ball, 80
  Zitumbuwa (Banana Fritters), 73
AIDS, 8, 67, 116, 117
Ancient Egypt, v, 5, 16, 32–34
animals
  hunting, 23, 24, 27, 29, 39–43, 48, 50, 67, 100
  livestock, 28, 29, 33, 34–35, 44–45, 52–55, 56, 58, 60, 66, 68, 100, 116
  migration of, 24
  myths/stories about, 106–109
  in Nile River basin, 6
  in rainforest, 7–9
  in Sahara Desert, 7
  on savannas, 22–29
  threats to, 29

apartheid, 20, 115–116
art, 14, 33, 36, 37, 47, 48, 57, 63, 71, 85. *See also* jewelry/ adornments; masks; music
Asante people, vi, 14, 37, 71, 83, 85, 113

## B

Bantu people, v, 52
baskets/bowls, 69, 70, 71–72, 74
Benin, Kingdom of, vi, 36, 85
buffalo, 25
Bushmen, 42

## C

Cape buffalo, 25
cattle, 29, 33, 34–35, 44–45, 52–55, 56, 58, 66, 68
cave paintings, 57
ceremonies/rituals, 47–48, 51, 53, 54, 55, 71, 77, 83, 88, 90, 95–102
challenges in Africa, 111–118
children, 44, 51, 53, 55, 60, 65–68, 72, 75–80, 95–97, 117
civilizations, v–vi, 2, 5, 16, 32–37, 85
climate, 6–7, 116–117
cloth/clothing, 37–38, 48, 81–84, 86, 96–97, 110
colonization, vi, 37, 104, 113–115

## D

daily life, 65–72
death/funerals, 16, 34, 71, 97–98, 99, 100
deforestation, 8, 20
diamonds, vi, 13, 18–20
disease, 8, 61, 67, 116, 117

## E

education, 66, 106, 115, 118
Egypt, Ancient, v, 5, 16, 32–34
elephants, 25–26, 106
environmental issues, 20, 29, 117
ethnic groups
  generally, 47–48, 49–58, 113–114
  Asante people, vi, 14, 37, 71, 83, 85, 113
  Bantu people, v, 52, 57
  Bushmen, 42
  Fang people, 100
  Kikuyu people, 44, 85, 101
  Maasai people, 44, 52–56, 58, 84, 85, 89, 95, 96–97
  Ndebele people, 63, 76
  San people, v, vi, 43, 50–52, 57, 91, 104
  Zulu people, 76, 84, 87, 104
Europeans in Africa, vi, 17, 20, 23, 29, 36, 37, 52, 57, 104, 112–115

## F

families, 43–44, 53–56, 60, 66–68, 70, 72
farmers/farming, 5, 33, 34–35, 43–44, 47, 67–68, 98, 100, 112, 116–117
fish/fishing, 5, 6, 67
food, 67–73. *See also* farmers/ farming; fish/fishing; herders/ herding; hunters/hunting
fossils, 2, 11
fufu, 69–70, 73
funerals/death, 16, 34, 71, 97–98, 99, 100

121

# INDEX

## G

games/toys, 75–80
geology, 10–11, 18–19
gold, vi, 13, 14, 16–18, 33, 37, 112
Great Rift Valley, 10–11
Great Zimbabwe kingdom, v, 34–35

## H

herders/herding, 44–45, 52–55, 56, 68, 100, 116
hippopotamus, 27
homes, 43, 50, 54, 59–64
hunters/hunting, 23, 24, 27, 29, 39–43, 48, 50, 67, 100

## I

independence, vi, 36, 37, 114–115
iron, 14–15

## J

jewelry/adornments, 14, 16, 21, 33, 36, 53, 55, 58, 84–85, 87, 96–97

## K

kente cloth, 37, 82, 83, 86
Kikuyu people, 44, 85, 101
Kingdom of Benin, vi, 36, 85

## L

language, 26, 34, 51, 103–105
leopards, 27–28, 107
lifestyle, 65–72
lions, 23–24

## M

Maasai people, 44, 52–56, 58, 84, 85, 89, 95, 96–97
Mandela, Nelson, 116
Mapfumo, Thomas (Lion of Zimbabwe), 92
maps, 3, 5, 9
marriage/weddings, 53, 54, 55, 76, 84, 90, 97
masks, 31, 47, 98–100, 102
metals, vi, 13–18, 33, 37, 112
migration, v, 20, 24
minerals, vi, 13–20, 33, 37, 112
mining, 16, 18–20, 114
Mount Kilimanjaro, 11
music, 51, 54, 72, 88–94

## N

natural wonders, 4–11
Ndebele people, 63, 76
Ngorongoro Crater, 10
Nile River, 4–6, 33

## P

people of Africa. See civilizations; ethnic groups
plants
   farming, 5, 33, 43–44, 67, 98, 100, 112, 116–117
   in rainforest, 7–9, 12
   in Sahara Desert, 7
   on savannas, 22
pottery, 71–72
poverty, 116–118

## R

rainfall, 6–7, 10, 24, 45, 116
rainforest, 7–9, 12
rhinoceros, 28
rivers, 4–6, 10, 33

## S

Sahara Desert, 6–7
San people, v, vi, 43, 50–52, 57, 91, 104
schools, 66, 106, 115
slavery/slave trade, v–vi, 36, 37, 112–113
Soyinka, Wole, 107
stories/storytelling, 44, 51, 52, 53, 57, 66, 72, 77, 105–110

## T

timeline of history, v–vi
tools, v, 14, 26, 35, 42, 62
trade, v–vi, 17, 19, 32, 34–35, 36, 37, 45, 72, 112–113, 115
tribes. See ethnic groups

## V

Victoria Falls, 9–10
volcanoes, 10–11, 18–19

## W

wars, 19, 55, 114, 116
water, 4–7, 9–10, 24, 33, 45, 61, 65–66, 71, 116–117
weapons, 14, 19, 39–42, 40–42, 55, 112
weather. See climate
World Cup, 80

## Z

Zimbabwe kingdom, Great, v, 34–35
Zulu people, 76, 84, 87, 104